°Boni

Maurice K.

Dec. 1ˢᵗ 1937.

CHAMPLIN ON FINE GRAIN

by

Harry Champlin

CAMERA CRAFT PUBLISHING COMPANY

425 Bush Street   San Francisco, Calif.

Copyright 1937

Camera Craft Publishing Company

San Francisco

First Edition

First Printing, February, 1937

Second Printing, June, 1937

PRINTED IN THE UNITED STATES OF AMERICA

BY

THE MERCURY PRESS, SAN FRANCISCO

Foreword

Introduction 8

Vast improvement in cameras and film.
Principal causes of failure.

Chapter One 11

Darkroom Procedures.

Development a routine procedure.
Developing equipment. Check-up before development.
Care of the hands. Pre-soaking. Inspection during devel-
opment. Safe lights. Agitation. A worth while experiment.
Hardening—Stop bath—why required. Hardening baths
before development. The fixing bath. Dangers of variations
in temperatures of solutions. Washing. Drying. The drying
cabinet.

Chapter Two 24

Relation of Exposure to Development.

Exposure controls density. Development controls contrast.
Developing time must be adjusted to film characteristics.
Film speed ratings. Special characteristics of slow fine
grain films. Special characteristics of fast films. Pre-
fogging. What type of film to use. Correct exposure.

Chapter Three 31

Perform this experiment!

Chapter Four 34

Fine Grain Developers.

The problem of Fine Grain. Short-comings of early for-
mulas. Essential constituents of a developer and their
action. Analysis of present fine grain formulas. Formulas
discussed: D-76, D-76-d, Glycin, straight paraphenylene-
diamine, paraphenylenediamine plus tri-basic sodium phos-
phate or ammonium chloride, Sease No. 3, paraphenylene-
diamine-glycin-metol.

Chapter Five 48

Developing Developers.

> *The objective sought. Early formulas No. 5 and No. 6. The Champlin No. 7, No. 8, No. 10 recommended for commercial finishing. The Champlin No. 9. Experiments with nickel salts. No. 11 and No. 14. The Champlin No. 15, its action and characteristics.*

Chapter Six 91

Causes of Failure.

> *Impure water. Compounding of formulas. Keeping developers. Over-working developers. The Fixing Bath. Reticulation. Hardening. Drying. Loading the camera. Fresh film. Sources of supply.*

Appendix A 100

Amateur Films.

> *Table of comparative speed values. Table of development times for amateur films and emulsion speed values for D-76 and Champlin No. 15.*

Appendix B 106

Developing Formulas.

> *Formulas. Uses. Keeping qualities. Emulsion speed rating. Developing Times.*

Appendix C 117

> *General chemicals, raw materials and developing substances used in Fine Grain Developing Formulae.*

Advertisements 144

FOREWORD

Some time ago, I read an article by a disgruntled man. While yet young, he had decided to become a photographer; he wished to become a pictorialist. In his desire to make himself proficient in this field, he first studied the action of gelatin emulsions and the photochemical action of the haloid salts in conjunction with gelatin both from the physical and the chemical standpoint. When he had finished this preliminary work, he felt that he was prepared to start his career.

After studying this subject for several years, he gathered together all of his pictures and found that they were not only lacking from an artistic standpoint but also left much to be desired technically. His conclusion was that while he had approached one of these technical problems and made it the sum total of his research, he should have first trained as an artist, because an artist approaches the subject as a unit and gathers only such technical knowledge as he needs as part of the sum total of his endeavor.

Mr. Champlin's approach to this subject is not that of a scientist but that of an artist. Early he found that there were certain technical difficulties which hampered the artistic rendering of his pictures—certain deficiencies or inherent defects in the negatives, which as a pictorialist, he has endeavored to correct. The degree to which he has been successful can best be determined by the response of the artists.

He has done a grand job, and we are all proud to know a man who, in spite of harsh criticism from the "unbelievers," has dared to produce negatives which for the first time allow us a better conception of "fine grain" and "quality."

J. P. SAMPSON, M. D.

CHAMPLIN ON

FINE GRAIN

INTRODUCTION

Photography with a miniature camera is a science of the highest order. During the past ten years the miniature camera has been made an instrument of mechanical precision. Lenses for these little cameras are marvels of optical speed and definition. Film manufacturers have kept pace with the advances made in these miniature cameras and have brought forth emulsions of almost unbelievable light-sensitivity and color correction. Miniature photography is truly a science.

The first roll of film taken with a miniature camera will likely be a great disappointment to the proud owner of that camera. So much is expected from these little cameras with their marvelous lenses and excellent films, that this disappointment is probably greater than it really should be. The camera, lens, and film are not at fault; the fault actually lies either with the operator of the camera or in the processing of the film after the exposure was made.

The principal defects in miniature negatives are movement of the camera, incorrect exposure, and improper processing or developing. Movement of the camera is a very common defect in miniature negatives and the result is a definite lack of sharpness of the whole negative. This fault probably accounts for much adverse criticism of the miniature camera. Experience gained with thousands of rolls of miniature negatives has shown that very few people can hold any camera in their hand during an exposure of 1/25 of a second without some movement showing in the negative. This movement can be almost imperceptible and yet it will cause a slight softening of the definition of a negative. This statement will probably bring loud protests from many camera enthusiasts who have been taking pictures for years with large cameras at 1/25 of a second. They will say that they can hold their cameras perfectly steady during exposures of this speed and will probably produce pictures to prove it. If the negatives made by these photographers were enlarged to as many times their original size as miniature negatives are enlarged, they would certainly be surprised. The size of the camera has nothing whatsoever to do with this fault.

A shutter speed of not less than 1/100 of a second is recommended whenever any camera is to be held in the hand. An excellent practice is to set the shutter at 1/100 of a second and to vary the diaphragm of the lens in accordance with the light conditions. This practice will result in a much higher percentage of good negatives and will eliminate the idea that a larger camera would do better work.

Incorrect exposure is likewise a serious menace to good photography with a miniature camera. It is, in fact, a serious menace to good photography with any camera. If negatives are under-exposed, there will be a decided flatness or lack of brilliance to the final picture. Errors in exposure can be corrected by the proper use of a good exposure meter. An exposure meter should be a part of the equipment of every serious photographer, regardless of the camera size. In fact, the exposure meter should be a part of the camera and one firm, Carl Zeiss, has incorporated an exposure meter in one of the models of their Contax camera.

The processing or developing of a miniature negative is a simple procedure. It is exactly the same in principle as the development of a large negative. The tremendous strides made by the miniature camera have resulted in devices for every conceivable phase of photography. Small tanks have been made for those who wish to process or develop their own film. These tanks are ingenious little affairs with reels upon which the film is wound in the dark. After the reel is in the tank and the lid of the tank replaced, the dark room can be dispensed with. The solution for developing film can be poured into a light-tight aperture in the lid of the tank and when development time is completed, this solution can be poured off and replaced with a fixing bath. All that is required in this work is a certain amount of care. One does not have to be a chemist or a laboratory specialist to do this work, and it is really one of the chief joys of miniature photography. The man who uses one of these fine precision instruments and then allows some one else to develop his films and make his prints can never really hope to know the full measure of enjoyment of miniature photography.

The author is aware of the fact that there is a considerable variety of developing formulas given in this book. In order to make the book useful to the reader who is interested in experimenting in this field it was necessary to include something of the history of fine grain developers, and to trace the course of experiment and reasoning which brought the Champlin formulas into being.

The reader who is interested only in practical results is cautioned against the folly of continually changing from one developer to another, and is advised to confine his tests to the Champlin #15 formula. The writer knows that this is his best formula, and is of the opinion that it is the best fine grain developer available to the miniature photographer today.

CHAPTER ONE

Dark-Room Procedure

The development of miniature negatives is a routine procedure. It is no different from the developing process used for any negative, regardless of size. More care must be exercised, however, because the negative is so small, and special fine grain formulas should be used. In actual practice all that the miniature photographer has to do is to take a suitable developing formula and insert the film in it. After a certain definite time has elapsed, the film should be rinsed in a bath compounded of certain chemicals so that the chemicals carried in the film from the developer will be neutralized. After the rinse in the stop bath, the negatives should be fixed in a good combination hardening-fixing solution. All that remains after these operations have been completed is the final wash to rid the film of all chemicals.

Miniature negative development is really one of the joys of miniature photography. It is definitely not an art filled with many deep mysteries. It does, however, require a maximum of care if satisfactory results are to be obtained. Before going further, we must understand clearly that miniature camera negatives have to be enlarged to many times their original size. Any defects such as scratches, dust, or pin holes will be enlarged also. These defects can be corrected by retouching the final print, but they can be avoided completely through the exercise of care and cleanliness.

Roll films are best developed in one of the small tanks

made especially for this purpose. The tank consists of a light-tight affair containing a reel upon which the film is wound. The reels are spirals so that the film can be wound without touching and so that there will be a free access of developer to all parts of the film. The lids of these tanks fit snugly and usually are made with an opening so that solutions can be poured in or out without allowing any light to enter.

The films are removed from the camera and wound upon the reel in the dark. The reel is then inserted in the tank and the tank covered with the lid. All subsequent operations can be conducted in a light room. Where several films are to be developed at one time in a dark room, the best method is to have several reels. All of the loaded reels are put into a pyrex beaker of developer. Pyrex beakers are obtainable from chemical and scientific supply houses. The beaker should be wide enough inside to hold the reel and high enough to accommodate as many reels as are desired for one developing. A stainless steel heavy gauge wire should be used upon which to string the reels so that they can be lifted in and out of the tank altogether. This wire should naturally be formed so that the bottom reel will not slip off.

Tanks and reels are made of either a composition such as bakelite or of stainless steel. Some reels have a celluloid apron which is used for proper separation of the film instead of the spiral. Stainless steel reels and tanks are generally more satisfactory; they are unbreakable and unaffected by the solutions used in processing film. A very satisfactory reel of this type is one made in this country called the Nikor, made of stainless steel. Three of these Nikor reels will fit nicely into a 1500 cc pyrex beaker, while a 2000 cc beaker will hold four reels.

Before commencing the development of a roll of negatives, be absolutely sure that the temperature of the solution is correct. If it is too low, it can be brought up by heating with an immersion type tumbler heater, ob-

Prof. A. D. Keller

Eastman Super X, exposed at Weston 40.

Developed in Champlin #7.

"The #7 formula has been used in the camera class of the University of California at Los Angeles for one year with splendid results."

—A. D. Keller, Prof. of Photography, U. C. L. A.

tainable from any electric supply house, or by any other means. If the temperature is too high, the solution should be cooled. This is best accomplished by pouring the solution into a bottle and setting the bottle into a container of cold water. Have the other solutions to be used after development, such as the stop bath and the fixing bath, ready. If films are to be developed in beakers, it is best to have three of these, one for the developing solution, one for the stop bath, and one for the fixing bath. If single reels of film are to be developed, this should be done in a tank. After the film has been loaded into the tank and the lid fitted over the tank, pour the developer into the aperture provided for this purpose. The tank should then be placed in a tray or other receptacle because with agitation there will be a certain seepage of developer and this will probably stain your hands and anything it touches. These stains are almost impossible to remove. This is specially true if paraphenylenediamine is used as a reducing agent. Any developer which spills out of the tray should be wiped up immediately and the place washed with soap and water. The hands should be washed with a mild alkaline soap such as that made by the Pacific Coast Borax Company and sold under the trade name "Boraxo."

It is not necessary to soak the film in clear water prior to developing. Soaking the film prior to development will naturally have a slight softening effect upon the gelatin and naturally some of the chemical elements will be dissolved out into the soaking water. Pre-soaking was advocated as a cure for air-bells which have a habit of forming upon the surface of the film and preventing the developer from acting upon the film behind them. A much better way to rid the film of these air-bells is to agitate the film thoroughly at given intervals during the process of development. If films are soaked thoroughly in clear water prior to development, the developing time will naturally be decreased slightly. Any other

14

advantage gained by prior soaking is of doubtful value.

After the films have been in the developer for two or three minutes, it is possible, with care, to inspect them by the light of a suitable safelamp. With a developer containing paraphenylenediamine, there is a slight desensitizing action, and this desensitizing action will allow a careful worker to use a safelight in the dark room. Extreme care must be exercised, however, if fog, due to exposure of super-sensitive material to light, is to be prevented. The desensitizing action of certain dyes, such as paraphenylenediamine, are of a distinct advantage because they prevent a certain amount of chemical fog and light fog from forming upon the surface of the film during visual inspection. The selection of a safelamp for this use should be made with care. A Kodak Safelamp fitted with either an Eastman Series 3 Panchromatic Safelight or an Agfa Super-sensitive Panchromatic Safelight, is recommended for use with ultra-rapid panchromatic film emulsions. The lamp should not exceed ten watts. Any light leakage around the glass or the opening for the glass should be sealed with adhesive tape.

Inspection of a film is a worth while practice because developers used in miniature camera work are used over and over again. Now, developers do break down. This is an unalterable law of photographic chemistry and inspection by the light of a suitable safelamp will tell whether or not development is proceeding as it should. To inspect a film requires a little experience. Different films behave differently in a developer and all developers do not build up contrast exactly alike. To learn something about the appearance of a negative during the stages of development, one should take a roll of film of one subject and made at the correct exposure. This film should be developed in the developer considered best suited to the worker's individual needs. If the developing time for proper contrast with this developer is, for example, fifteen minutes, the film should be inspected every two minutes and after ten minutes have elapsed, one or two frames should be cut from the roll and dropped into the fixing bath. This procedure should be duplicated every minute until the film is used up. Each time the density of the image should be noticed and the films should be so separated in the fixing bath that they can be identified. After the negatives have been cleared in the fixing bath, their densities can be compared with the density of image noted by inspection under the safelight. Inspections of films during the process of development is not entirely necessary because there are times and temperature tables for each developer. It is, however, a good practice to inspect a film at the end of the correct developing time. Inspection should be made of just a few frames. If the densities appear correct, the film can be fixed; if they are not correct, the film should be developed longer. Do not attempt to handle the reel or film with the bare hands if the developer contains paraphenylenediamine. This practice may lead to a bad staining of the hands which can be removed only by the process of time.

During the process of development the film should be agitated every two minutes or so to prevent the formation of air-bells and streaks due to uneven development. The best method is to divide the total developing time into ten parts so that the film will be agitated at evenly spaced intervals ten times during the process of development. For example, if the total developing time is twenty minutes, agitate every two minutes. This is the only way in which accuracy can be assured. Ordinary roll film need not be agitated so often because this film has no sprocket holes along the edges. The sprocket holes of 35 mm film will cause definite streaks of light and dark along one edge of the film if it is not agitated sufficiently during development. Continuous agitation is, of course, the best and will cause a decrease in developing time. This decrease in developing time usually amounts to about twenty per cent of the times given.

After development has been completed, pour off the solution and refill the tank with a solution consisting of:

Water	16 ounces	500 ccs
Sodium Bisulphite	109 grains	7 grams
Potassium Chrome Alum	109 grains	7 grams

It is not necessary to weigh these chemicals with the utmost precision; in fact, we can use a half teaspoonful of each in the specified quantity of water.

This bath will stop development instantly. It will also harden the film completely so that there will be much less chance of any harm occurring to the emulsion surface during subsequent operations. This bath should be used because the chemicals in all fine grain formulas will quickly break down a fresh hardening-fixing solution. This is particularly true if the developer contains paraphenylenediamine and glycin. The breakdown of a hardening-fixing bath is not apparent and yet it is very serious because it permits undue swelling of the gelatin in the fixing bath and final wash, and sometimes reticulation results. Reticulation is serious and means that the gelatin of the emulsion has swollen so far that its structure has been affected and upon drying, it contracts into an irregularly shaped series of wrinkles. For this reason a stop bath should always be used between developing and fixation. The stop bath will neutralize some of the chemicals carried in the film from the developer to the fixing bath. In addition to this neutralizing effect, there will be a decided hardening which is due to the potassium chrome alum. This chemical is one of the best gelatin hardeners, but its life is very short. For this reason it is wise to use a fresh stop bath for each batch of films developed. *At the most, the stop bath should not be used longer than one day.*

The use of a hardening bath prior to development is a practice to be thoroughly discouraged. No gelatin hardener will completely harden film and make it impervious to water. If we harden a film and then leave it in water long enough, it will soften. A pre-hardening bath prevents softening of the gelatin by the developer to the extent that the developer cannot penetrate the film and properly attack all of the light-affected silver. By the time the film reaches the final wash, some of the effects of the pre-hardening have begun to wear off and the film is not fully protected from possible injury. Formalin and formaldehyde are the chemicals generally used in pre-hardening and these chemicals are responsible for considerable fog, streaks in the developed image, and some loss of shadow detail. This last fault is caused by the inability of the developer to thoroughly penetrate the gelatin and reduce all of the light-affected silver particles in the weaker portions of the negative. If potassium chrome alum is used as a pre-hardening bath, there is an ever-present danger that the effects of this chemical will be counteracted by some chemical in the developer and this counteraction might result in reticulation.

Films should be agitated in the stop bath. There is a tendency for potassium chrome alum to deposit a slight chemical sludge upon the surface of an emulsion. This deposit will not occur if the films are agitated. Films can be left in the stop bath for from thirty seconds to three minutes. The actual length of time is unimportant although it should not be less than thirty seconds. The stop bath should then be poured off and the fixing bath poured into the tank.

The fixing bath is used to dissolve out of the film all of the silver which was not light-affected and then reduced by the developing solution. A good fixing bath is one compounded with plain hypo crystals and Velox liquid hardener in the proportions recommended by the Eastman Kodak Company. For those who prefer to mix their own solution, the regular hypo-sulphite-acetic acid-alum bath is recommended. This bath is as follows:

Eastman Formula F-5

Water	16	ounces	500	ccs
Hypo	8	ounces	240	ccs
Sodium Sulphite	½	ounce	15	grams
Acetic Acid 28% pure	1½	fluid ounces	48	ccs
Boric Acid crystals	¼	ounce	7.5	grams
Potassium Alum	½	ounce	15	grams
Water to make	32	ounces	1	litre

18

Dissolve the chemicals in the order given. This bath should be made up in advance because the dissolving of hypo in water lowers the temperature of the water. The temperature of the fixing bath need not be as carefully maintained as the temperature of the developer; in fact, experiments conducted by Harry Crawford have shown that with paraphenylenediamine-glycin developers it is possible to plunge the film from a developer of 72° Fahrenheit to a fixing bath of 62° Fahrenheit without harm. This is contrary to most of the advice given miniature camera workers. The most serious change in processing is a change from a low temperature to a high temperature. This change is very serious and should not be made because it will be harmful to the film.

The amateur photographer is strongly advised against maintaining the different solutions used in development at different temperatures. Gelatin is really a weak substance and care and common sense should be exercised with it. When gelatin is immersed in water, it absorbs water and swells, and the rate of absorption and swelling are in proportion to the temperature of the water. If the water temperature is high, the gelatin will swell more, while if the temperature is low, it will absorb less water, and consequently the swelling will decrease. From this it will be seen that changes in temperature will materially affect the gelatin, and if the changes in temperature are beyond a few degrees, the gelatin may expand or contract with such rapidity that the structure of the gelatin is materially affected.

The best fixing bath for general use with miniature cameras is one made fresh for each day's run of films. A bath which works perfectly and with a minimum of time is made as follows:

| Water | 16 ounces | 500 ccs |
| Hypo | 4 ounces | 120 grams |

Dissolve completely, then add:

Sodium Bisulphite	150 grains	10 grams
Potassium Chrome Alum	150 grains	10 grams
Ammonium Chloride	½ ounce	14 grams

In preparing this fixing bath, dissolve one pint (480 grams) of plain hypo crystals in one-half gallon (2 litres) of water. This will be a stock solution. For use, take sixteen ounces of this solution and add the other ingredients to it. Films will fix perfectly and be fully hardened in this solution in about ten minutes. This fixing bath should be used and then discarded. This is probably the safest way for the miniature camera photographer to fix his films and if this bath is used, the stop bath can be dispensed with. After fixation the films should be washed in running water in order to remove all of the hypo and other chemicals from the emulsion. The minimum time required under the most efficient washing conditions will be from fifteen to twenty minutes, but the safest washing time for the amateur photographer is from forty minutes to one hour. If films are not properly washed, there will be a continued action by the chemicals in the emulsion and sooner or later the films will be a total loss.

The film has now been completely developed, fixed, and washed, and may be removed from the reel. A clip should be fastened to each end and the film hung up for wiping. The best type of film clip is one with a couple of teeth which penetrate through the film. The ends of the film should be doubled over so that they will not break loose from the clip. In wiping the film use either a viscose sponge or a chamois. For all practical purposes the chamois is perfectly satisfactory for general use. It should be kept in a jar of water and never allowed to dry out. The film should be wiped by wringing the chamois dry and drawing it down hard over the film. This will not scratch the film unless through carelessness the chamois or viscose sponge has been allowed to collect grit. Be sure that the film is wiped surface dry so that no water spots or streaks are left on either side. After wiping the film, hang it up to dry. Some workers advocate spraying the film with distilled water after developing. This practice has advantages, but it is not neces-

"Clark Gable and Director John Stahl"   Rex Hardy
Courtesy Time, Inc. and Life.

Contax with F:1.5 Sonnar; DuPont Superior exposed at Weston 32, by Mazda light. Developer, Champlin #15.

"Modern high speed photography would be impossible without modern high speed lenses in combination with high speed emulsions. The advantages derived from this combination would in turn be void without a modern high speed developer."
—Rex Hardy

sary. A thorough wiping of the surface of the film with a chamois will remove all moisture and the sediment in the moisture just as thoroughly without the distilled water.

Grain size will be affected by the length of time required to dry a film. Film should be dried if possible in about thirty minutes. If too long a time is taken for this part of the processing of the film, there will be some agglomeration or bunching of the reduced silver grains in the emulsion. Likewise, if drying is too rapid, there will be additional turbulence created within the emulsion and agglomeration of the grains will result. The best way to dry film is to make a metal lined cabinet just large enough to hold the strips of film and to force warm air through this cabinet with a small heating fan. Such an arrangement is inexpensive and most satisfactory. The heat from the fan should be turned off as soon as the films are thoroughly dried. If the films are subjected to a warm air fan for too long a period, there is a possibility that they will become too brittle and will require reconditioning with glycerine and water. Once drying has commenced at a certain temperature, do not change that temperature because there will be an unevenness of drying and this will surely show in the film.

After processing the films, be sure to clean the tank and other containers immediately. Any developer which spilled out of the tank into the tray can be poured back into the bottle if it was not contaminated with either the stop bath or fixing bath. If so much as one drop of either of these baths spilled into the tray, this surplus developer should be discarded.

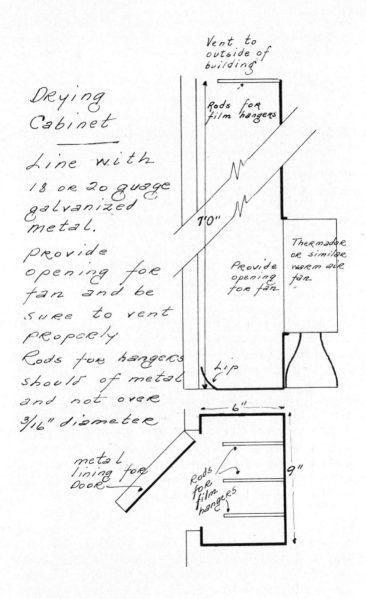

Vent to
outside of
building

Drying
Cabinet

Line with
18 or 20 guage
galvanized
metal.

Provide
opening for
fan and be
sure to vent
properly

Rods for hangers
should of metal
and not over
3/16" diameter

Rods for
film hangers

7'0"

Provide
opening
for fan

Thermador
or similar
warm air
fan.

Lip

metal
lining for
Door

6"

Rods
for
film
hangers

9"

CHAPTER TWO

Relation of Exposure to Development

In developing any film it is well to remember that the density of the resulting negative will be in direct proportion to the amount of exposure that negative received, and the contrast of the negative will depend entirely upon the length of time that negative was allowed to remain in the developer. Density of the negative is a result of exposure, while contrast is the result of development. These two facts are not fully understood by the majority of amateur photographers. If a negative lacks shadow detail, that negative did not receive proper exposure. If a negative does not have sufficient contrast, it was not developed long enough, while if it has too much contrast, it was developed too long. Some films develop rapidly and are capable of giving extreme contrast in a short developing time, while other films develop slowly and the contrast must be built up by prolonged development. As a general rule, slow fine grain films develop rapidly and are capable of giving much greater contrast than the ultra-rapid type of films. The contrast of a film is something entirely aside from the density of a film.

The density of a film determines whether or not there is a sufficient deposit in the weaker portions to give full shadow detail in a print. The exposure of a film is the one factor governing the density of that film. This fact can not be stressed too highly. In exposing any film, due consideration must be made of the type and special characteristics of that film. This is particularly true with miniature films because a slight error in exposure may completely change the tone scale of the resulting negative.

Film manufacturers do not all use a standard method of determining the speed of their emulsions. Each manufacturer uses a different system in arriving at emulsion speed and these ratings are usually based upon highlight detail. In other words, these ratings usually indicate the minimum exposure requirements of the emulsion. These ratings are not actually an indication of the speed of an emulsion and should not be used as such. For example, some fine grain films actually require at least fifty per cent more exposure than a highlight speed rating would indicate.

With the list of films in another section of this book, Weston speed ratings are given, for D-76 and Champlin #15 in daylight, and for Champlin #15 in Mazda light. A conversion table is also supplied for translating the Weston ratings into H. & D., Scheiner, or DIN ratings.

Slow fine grain 35 mm films should actually be given at least fifty per cent more exposure than the manufacturers' speed ratings would indicate. Slow fine grain films were created in response to a demand by the motion picture industry for an emulsion with a fine grain and sufficient contrast for the enormous enlargements required by the industry in background work. These films develop rapidly and build up an extreme contrast which may be nice to look at but is very difficult to print. The developing time of a slow fine grained film should be less than is usually given by the amateur photographer. This is not really under-developing because slow fine grain films are usually over-developed.

When films are inserted in a developing solution, the developer penetrates the emulsion and gradually changes the silver halide to black metallic silver. The longer the film is in the developing solution, the more silver halide grains will be reduced to black metallic silver. Film emulsions do not record both highlight and shadow detail in the same proportion as seen by the human eye. The emulsion will be greatly affected by a strong highlight, and a weak light emanating from a deep shadow will have very little effect upon the emulsion. If films are allowed to remain in a developer long enough to develop the full intensity of the highlight which had a strong effect upon the light-sensitive silver, this intensity will be so great that it will completely ruin the printing value of the weak shadow.

Subjects in extremely poor light condition can best be photographed with pre-fogged film. This is an old practice and yet one about which little is known. The principle underlying this practice is based upon the fact that there is an initial inertia to a film emulsion. This means that a certain amount of light is necessary to start the change in the silver halide which takes place during exposure. If film is pre-fogged, given a slight even coating of fog by exposure to an even weak light, this initial inertia will be overcome. Any additional light then will be recorded fully upon the film. For this reason pre-fogged film will record a much greater wealth of weak shadow detail than will films which have not been pre-fogged. Pre-fogging of film is a subject about which much will be said in the next year or two. It may be that the film manufacturers will pre-fog film for use in newspaper and other work which can not wait for good and proper light conditions.

The criterion of any negative is the print which can be made from it. If the highlights lack detail due to the fact that the silver deposit in the negative is too great, then it is safe to say that the negative was over-developed. There must be a perfect balance in a negative between the densities of the highest light and the deepest shadow in which detail is desired. Slow fine grain films are usually under-exposed and then developed to the point where the highlight detail is very dense.

Prints from these negatives have to be made upon very soft working paper and even then they have somewhat of a soot and chalk appearance. The proper way to use any slow fine grain film is to give at least fifty per cent more exposure than the manufacturer's speed rating would indicate. This will give full shadow detail. These films should then be given less development and this will prevent the over-exposed highlights from building up to an extreme density. If this practice is followed, slow fine grain films will give nicely graded negatives with full shadow detail and a splendid delicacy of tones in the highlights.

Modern ultra-rapid film emulsions should be given a minimum exposure and full development. Ultra-rapid films are very soft working. The shadow detail is recorded easily and these films do not have a tendency toward over-exposure in the highlights. The contrast is nearer that recorded by the human eye. For this reason these films should be developed for a long time in order that sufficient contrast or tonal difference between highlight and shadow may be built up. If an ultra-rapid film is over-exposed to any appreciable extent, shadow detail will be built up to the extent that there will be very little difference between the highlights and the shadows, and a very flat picture will result. Too many amateur photographers try to over-expose and under-develop a film because they were told that this was the correct way to secure fine grain negatives. In so doing, all contrast and tone quality is sacrificed.

There are, then, two distinct types of film emulsions generally used by miniature camera workers. To understand the difference between these two types requires some knowledge of the characteristics of these films. Slow films are generally finer grained than fast films, and naturally, fast films are coarser grained than slow films. So far, it has not been possible for film manufacturers to create an emulsion combining high speed and ultra fine grain. When light strikes one particle of silver in an emulsion, it is deflected to the surrounding particles. We all know that if we have two mirrors, one large and one small, the large one will reflect much more light than will the small one. Hence, it will be seen that the deflection of light from one small particle of silver will not cover as great an area as will the light deflected from a large particle. It follows then that much more light must fall upon a given area of film containing microscopically fine grains of silver than will be required upon a film of coarse grains in order to affect so much light-sensitive silver. Slow films are made with fine particles of silver salts, while fast films are made with coarser particles of silver salts. There are, of course, other more actual reasons why certain films are faster than other films. There are sensitizing dyes and other feats of chemistry which are responsible for the tremendous differences in speeds of emulsions. It is not necessary to dwell upon these in this book.

There is no actual mystery to correct exposure and correct development. The manufacturers of film emulsions furnish a speed indication of their films and this indication can be used to determine the correct exposure of the film. To this indication should be added knowledge gained through experiments with the actual type of light conditions upon which the film is to be used. If the light has great contrast, with brilliant highlights and deep shadows, slow fine grain films should be used. These films should be exposed so that detail in the shadows will be present in the finished negatives. This detail can only be the result of sufficient exposure. The contrast built up in developing these slow films will take care of the over-exposure so that the result will not be flat and uninteresting. On the other hand, if there is little contrast in the scene, such as shots from an airplane or desert photography, slow films should be used. Here again the contrast gained in developing these films will build up so that there will be sufficient contrast in the final print. For almost all other work ultra-rapid emulsions will give the most satisfactory results. With these ultra-rapid films there is an ever-present danger of over-exposure and flatness. For this reason these films should receive a minimum exposure. Ultra-rapid films record both highlight and shadow detail better than slow films, and the result is more nearly that seen by the human eye.

In developing films these is one standard time which will give correct tone scale to a negative. This time factor is based upon the length of time necessary for the reducing agents in the developer to reduce the silver halide to metallic silver. If this time factor is varied one way or the other, there will be a difference in the contrast of the resulting negative. If the developing time is decreased, the negative will have less contrast, while if it is increased, it will have more contrast. A properly developed negative is one which will print upon a medium grade paper. There will be detail in the highlights and also in the shadows. If contrast paper or soft paper is needed to print highlight and shadow detail, the negative was improperly exposed or developed. If a properly exposed negative is developed so that it will print perfectly upon a medium grade of paper, we can safely assume that the correct emulsion speed of that film and the correct development time for the negative were both ascertained. We should make all negatives to print on medium paper because medium paper is the only paper which will show the longest tone scale. All other papers lack something. To make either soft or hard papers, manufacturers are forced to shorten one end or other of the tone scale of that paper. It follows then that a negative which will print best on medium paper will have the longest tone scale and the one with a long tone scale is the one which received correct exposure and was correctly developed. If slow films are exposed at the speeds generally utilized by miniature camera workers and developed in the gosh-awful manner that characterizes so many miles of film, they will certainly not print on medium paper. This means that they have been incorrectly exposed and incorrectly developed. Now, some workers develop all their negatives so that they will print on soft bromide paper and this is a very serious mistake because soft bromide paper will never give the brilliant results that can be obtained only with medium paper. This is contrary to a great many miniature camera workers' beliefs, but it is true.

The time required for a negative to reach correct contrast depends upon the developer used and the temperature of the solution. Correct negatives are a result of a standardization of developing time and the idea that each and every negative in a roll should actually receive separate treatment is an old one which should be discarded. If negatives are correctly exposed and developed for the correct length of time required to bring them to proper contrast, all negatives in a roll will print on medium paper and this is as it should be. Where there are great variations in densities of the negatives in a roll, there is an inconsistency in exposure, and no variation in the developing time will correct this because the density of a negative is a function of exposure. If the contrast of a negative is incorrect for printing on medium paper, then there is a fault in developing. If the contrast is too great, the developing time should be decreased; if the contrast is too little, the developing time should be increased. The contrast of a negative is solely a result of the development of that negative. Developing times are lengthened with fine grain developers and with other developers because these developers are used over and over again and they do wear out. This breakdown of the developer necessitates an increase in time in order to bring the negatives to full contrast. This is the only reason why negatives should be inspected. Inspection of a negative should not be used to correct errors in exposure.

CHAPTER THREE

Perform This Experiment!

The only way to do good work in photography is to know your camera and lens, your film emulsion, and your developer. Only by a perfect coordination of all of these units can there be any real perfection. Many amateur photographers are fuly aware of the capabilities and limitations of their camera and lens. They know less about their films, and much less about the developing solutions they use. There should be some understanding of the actual capabilities of a film with a given developing solution. So many films and so many developing solutions are used because some one else uses them or because some one said they were good or because some one wanted to sell them. The only real way to determine whether or not a developer is suited to the film you are using and to the subjects you are photographing is by actual test. Such a test can be made simply, and should be made by every one really interested in photography.

A series of exposures should be made ranging from correct exposure to three stops less than correct exposure and to three stops more than correct exposure. This series of exposures should be developed in the formula selected for general use. After the negatives have been fixed and washed and dried, they should be examined carefully for shadow detail and printing quality. A negative that looks nice is not always the best printing negative; in fact, miniature negatives that look nice are usually worthless. Miniature negatives should be delicate, with a wealth of detail in the shadows, and highlights not so dense as to block up in printing. The final print is the criterion by which any developing solution should be judged. The shadow detail determines whether or not the combination of film and developer have correct emulsion speed. The reader of this book is advised to make a test with his favorite film and favorite developing solution upon the subject he enjoys photographing. A second test should be made with the same film and formula No. 15 given in this book. This test will show that there is a difference in developers. This test should be made with every change in developing formula, for only by a direct and honest comparison can a true realization of the difference between developers be attained.

A good developing formula is one combining not only fine grain and emulsion speed but tone quality as well. A miniature negative is so small that differences in tone values are difficult to detect with the human eye. The tests should be carried through to projection prints.

In judging a film-developer combination, it is necessary, of course, that the films should be correctly developed. Films that are correctly developed will have no highlight that is so dense as to be unprintable without sacrificing shadows. Our eye is able to penetrate highlights and to see detail in them. Our eye is also able at the same time to see a certain amount of shadow detail. The graduation between the deepest shadow and the highest light of a print should be gradual and delicate, and not rapid and harsh as is the case with so many miniature prints. If the negative which appears to meet these requirements best is more or less than the normal exposure called for by the light conditions of the scene photographed, then that is the correct emulsion speed

"Insignia for the Club"   *Will Connell*

Developed in Champlin #7

"The Champlin theories of development are definitely a step toward emulsion speed and fine grain."

—Will Connell

of the film-developer combination. The film-developer combination requiring the least exposure and giving the finest grain is the one which should be used.

CHAPTER FOUR

Fine Grain Developers

To deal intelligently with the subject of grain in a negative, there must be some understanding of the problem. In the manufacture of an emulsion, silver nitrate and either potassium or ammonium bromide are mixed together and the resulting precipitate is the light-sensitive silver halide in the film. During the exposure in the camera light strikes this sensitive silver salt and it is deflected as if by a series of prisms or mirrors from one silver salt particle to another. Hence, light will affect not only the silver salt particle upon which it falls, but also some of the surrounding particles will become affected. The light causes a certain change in the silver salt and makes it possible for a metallic silver to be formed during the process of development. The change which takes place in the silver salt is not actually known. All that is known is that there is a latent image formed in the emulsion. The metallic silver is formed during the process of development in direct proportion to the amount of light that strikes the emulsion during exposure. In the process of development all of the silver halide in the emulsion is stirred up and there is an attraction which causes the silver grains to gather together in little clumps or groups. These little groups or clumps are the grains which have been bothering the miniature camera world so much. The problem, then, is to reduce all of the light-affected halide to metallic silver without the bunching or agglomerating of these particles into irregularly spaced and shaped large particles.

The answer to this problem undoubtedly lies in the compounding of a developing formula which will reduce all of the light-affected silver halide to metallic silver and yet will effectively prevent this clumping of the silver grains. So far, this problem remains unsolved although the world has been deluged with suggestions as to just how this can be accomplished. Most of these suggestions have come from amateur photographers. Photographic chemists have not offered anything new or startling in the past ten years. There appears to be a strange similarity between all of the formulas offered the miniature camera section of the photographing public. Some formulas offered give very fine grained images because they do not reduce all of the light-affected silver halide to metallic silver nor do they have the power to act upon slightly affected silver grains. To secure full shadow detail with these developers, it is necessary to increase the exposure to make up for this deficiency. These formulas are truly a hindrance to the advancement of photography because they do not allow full use to be made of the speed of modern lenses and film emulsions. It seems perfectly silly to have a camera with a shutter speed of 1/1000 of a second, a lens with an effective aperture of f/1.5, and an ultra-rapid film emulsion if we cannot utilize all of this speed. Chemistry has not kept pace with the advances made by camera and film manufacturers.

Other formulas offered have the ability to shave the silver grains during the process of development until they are microscopically small. This idea originated about fifteen years ago and was an outstanding contribution at that time. The shaving of the silver grains naturally leaves voids in between the grains and these voids are just as serious as the clumping itself. In mak-

35

ing an enlargement from any negative, we have to project light through the negative and if the spaces between the silver grain which make up the image are large and irregular, they will surely show as large, black dots in the finished prints. This type of developing formula may reduce all of the light-affected silver and then shave all of the grains to a very small size, yet prints from negatives developed in these solutions can be very coarse grained and very disappointing, notwithstanding the fact that the actual grain size in the negative is microscopically small.

Now, a perfect fine grain developer should reduce all of the light-affected silver halide to metallic silver without allowing any movement of the silver grains within the gelatin. If the silver grains within the gelatin were not allowed to clump, there would be no problem whatsoever because the original silver halide is probably finer than the finest reduced metallic silver.

In compounding any developer we need, first, a reducing agent. Chemical reducers are agents with an affinity for oxygen. They have the power to reduce the light-affected silver to metallic silver without affecting the silver halide which has not been exposed to light. A reducing agent would have a very short life and be probably worthless unless a preservative were added to the developing solution because it would become oxidized before it could do any work. Sodium sulphite is the chemical generally used in developers as a preservative because it has a very strong affinity for oxygen. Sodium sulphite is readily oxidized to sodium sulphate and in drawing the oxygen to itself, this chemical protects the reducing agent from oxidizing so readily. A developer must be able to penetrate all the gelatin and attack all of the silver in the emulsion. Developers originally were compounded with strong alkalis such as sodium carbonate, ammonia, acetone, or the hydroxides because these strong alkalis have the power to break down the gelatin structure and allow free access to the organic chemical which has to do the reducing. This breakdown of the gelatin structure promotes the clumping of the silver grains into little groups. There is an actual attraction between silver grains, and if the gelatin in which these grains are imbedded is allowed to break down, there will be a natural movement of the silver grains toward one another. Before the advent of the miniature camera, this graininess due to this clumping was of no consequence whatsoever. Developers containing little or no free alkali do not have the power to break down the gelatin structure so completely and there is far less clumping of the silver grains.

It may be well for us to consider here some of the developing formulas which have been brought out with the idea of reducing grain size before going into experiments which were conducted and first announced in CAMERA CRAFT in August, 1936.

Sodium sulphite is the chemical generally used as a preservative in developers. Sodium sulphite oxidizes readily to sodium sulphate. This chemical can be used with water as a developer because it is an oxidizing agent. The concentration of sodium sulphite in such a developer must be near the saturation point. The reduction of the silver halide to metallic silver is naturally a result of the oxidation process of the sodium sulphite. A silver image obtained by this means will be weak and flat and practically worthless because sodium sulphite does not have the power to give a marked differentiation between exposed and unexposed silver. If an exposed film is left in a saturated solution of sodium sulphite for an indefinite time, an image will be developed, while if the film is left in this solution long enough, all of the silver will be dissolved out of the solution by the sodium sulphite. Sodium sulphite is a reducing agent but it is not sufficiently selective because it will attack the silver affected by light as well as that which was not affected by light. The action of sodium sulphite in its attack upon silver is to eat away slowly at the edges of the silver until there is nothing left. This action is the basis for the high concentration of sodium sulphite in so many fine grain developers. Sodium sulphite should be carbonate free; in other words, this chemical should be fairly pure and contain no free alkali. The addition of any alkali to a plain sodium sulphite solution will cause a heavy chemical fog.

When metol is added to a high concentration of sodium sulphite, the reducing action of the metol is greatly accelerated. If one, two, or three grams per litre (15, 30, 45 grains per 32 ounces) is added to a ten per cent sodium sulphite solution, we will have a developer capable of reducing all of the light-affected silver in the emulsion. The silver grains will be shaved to a microscopic size by the normal action of the sodium sulphite, and the voids in between will be large and irregular. The resulting negatives will make full graduation, coarse grained prints. The action of these two chemicals will be greatly speeded by the addition of a mild akali such as sodium borate (borax). The quantity of sodium borate used should be one or two grams per litre (15 to 30 grains for 32 ounces). The life of such a developer will be rather short and after the first roll of film is developed in it, it will be unstable.

Another organic reducing agent, hydroquinone, is usually aded to sodium sulphite-metol-sodium borate developers. This chemical does little or no actual reducing of the silver halide to metallic silver; it merely acts as a sort of buffer in the solution and also as a preservative of the other chemicals. There is a slight decrease in the graininess of a negative when developed in a metol-sodium sulphite-borax developer to which has been added a small quantity of hydroquinone. The borax type of developers have much to recommend them for average use with large negatives. These developers keep well and because they reduce all of the light-affected silver in the emulsion, exposures need be no more than called for by a properly used electric photometer. A good borax formula is the one advocated by the Eastman Kodak Company, the D-76 formula:

Eastman D-76

Elon (metol)	29	grains	2 grams
Sodium Sulphite	3½	ounces	100 grams
Hydroquinone	72	grains	5 grams
Sodium Borate (borax)	29	grains	2 grams
Water	32	ounces	1 litre

This type of developer has many variations. Some advocates of borax developers believe that the borax should be increased and the sodium sulphite decreased. Such a formula was brought out by Wellington in England many years ago. Later the Eastman Company made an extensive series of experiments and increased the amount of borax in their formula D-76 and added boric acid also. This is known as the buffered borax negative developing formula D-76-d:

Eastman D-76-d

Elon (metol)	29	grains	2 grams
Sodium Sulphite	3½	ounces	100 grams
Hydroquinone	72	grains	5 grams
Sodium Borate (borax)	120	grains	8 grams
Water	32	ounces	1 litre
Acid Boric, crystals	120	grains	8 grams

The developing time of the D-76 formula is from nine to twelve minutes at 65° Fahrenheit, and these times apply also to the D-76-d formula. It is possible to vary the developing time by changing the ratio between the sodium borate and boric acid. If the boric acid is too high, the life of this developer will be seriously impaired and the reduction ability likewise impaired. Sodium sulphite-metol-sodium borate formulas are not the answer to the fine grain developing problem confronting the miniature photographer. These developers do allow correct exposure, and for that reason they have an advantage over most of the fine grain formulas offered to miniature photographers. The grain structure of negatives developed in these formulas is too coarse for use in miniature camera work.

Another school of thought advocated the use of

chemical reducing agent glycin in place of metol. Glycin makes crystal clear solutions which do not create so much turbulence in the emulsion during the process of development. Negatives developed with glycin as the reducing agent have somewhat finer grain than negatives developed with metol. Glycin is comparatively dormant in the neutral sulphite solution generally used in fine grain work and really requires an alkali to stimulate it to activity. The alkali generally used with glycin is potassium carbonate. In developers containing glycin, sodium sulphite and potassium carbonate, the amount of sodium sulphite should not exceed the amount of glycin in the developer. If the sodium sulphite concentration is much higher than the glycin concentration, there will be a distinct chemical fog formed in the emulsion. This fog materially affects the printing value of the negative. A developer can be made up as follows:

Water	32 ounces	1 litre
Sodium Sulphite	6 grains	.5 gram
Glycin	6 grains	.5 gram
Potassium Carbonate	15 grains	1.2 grams

Developing time is three-quarters to one and one-half hours at 68° Fahrenheit. This developer will give negatives with a comparatively fine grain and great brilliance. The grain size is no improvement over that given by the formula D-76-d.

Some years ago paraphenylenediamine was brought to the attention of the photographic world because it gave very fine grained images when used in a highly concentrated sodium sulphite solution. This chemical, known to the fur-dyeing industry as Ursol D, gave a reddish brown image upon the negative. The action of such a developer was semi-physical; in other words, there was a deposit upon the latent image in combination with the actual development of the latent image. The grain structure of negatives developed with this reducing agent was so fine and so even that tremendous enlargements could be made without any troublesome grain. Moreover, there was a velvety quality to the half tones. The great disadvantage of this developer, however, was the enormous increase in exposure time necessary to produce correct shadow detail in the negative. Now, correct shadow detail in a negative is the criterion of its emulsion speed. If shadow detail is lacking, we can safely say that the film was under-exposed or that the developer did not reduce all of the silver halide to metallic silver. Paraphenylenediamine and sodium sulphite require about five times more exposure than formula D-76 in order to affect the silver halide sufficiently so that it can be reduced to metallic silver. This was a disadvantage far outweighing the fine grain properties of the developer. Still another disadvantage of this developer was the irregularity of the results produced by it. The keeping qualities of this developer were very poor. Paraphenylenediamine and sodium sulphite were, however, something entirely new in the way of fine grain developers and this fine grain developer was actually the first one which the amateurs could use with any degree of success.

Paraphenylenediamine and sodium sulphite dissolve a large quantity of silver out of the negative. This silver is acted upon by the developer and naturally causes a breakdown of the developer. This is true even when other reducing agents are combined in the developer in order that its reducing power might be increased. For this reason there is a definite loss in developing power whenever a roll of film is developed. This loss in developing power is in proportion to the area of film and the length of time the film is in the developer. These two factors are, naturally, very difficult to gauge with any accuracy and the developer is, therefore, unstable.

When paraphenylenediamine - sulphite developers were first revived a few years ago, some workers advocated the addition to the developer of mild alkalis in order that the reducing action might be accelerated. Tri-basic sodium phosphate was added. The reducing action was accelerated so that the emulsion speed was increased. The increase, however, was only 1.9 times the exposure required by formula D-76-d. This was hardly worth while because there was some increase in the grain structure and the emulsion speed was by no means normal. Still another addition was ammonium chloride. This chemical accelerated the reducing action more than tri-basic sodium phosphate. The use of ammonium chloride in developers is not new. This chemical has been used for at least twenty years. The effect of the ammonium chloride was more like a stronger alkali. This was due, of course, to the ammonia. These additions to paraphenylenediamine and sulphite were not the answer to the fine grain and high emulsion speed problem.

The addition of glycin to a paraphenylenediamine-sodium sulphite developer will have a stabilizing influence upon that developer. The glycin is not used as a reducing agent; in this case it is actually a buffer and a preservative of the paraphenylenediamine. When used with glycin, paraphenylenediamine has a greatly increased reducing power and this naturally results in an increase in film speed over a plain paraphenylenediamine-sodium sulphite developer. The quantity of glycin can be varied to suit individual requirements. The amount of glycin usually incorporated with paraphenylenediamine and sodium sulphite is from one-half to the full amount of paraphenylenediamine in that developer. The best known formula of this type is the Sease No. 3 formula:

Sease #3

Water	32 ounces	1 litre
Paraphenylenediamine	146 grains	10 grams
Sodium Sulphite	3 ounces	90 grams
Glycin	88 grains	6 grams

The emulsion speed of this developer is less than normal; in other words, this developer requires an exposure of 2.8 times that required by the D-76-d formula. The D-76-d formula can be taken as an indication of a

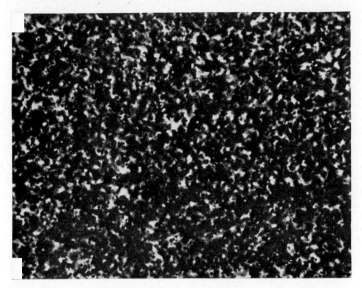

Photomicrograph of DuPont Superior film developed in Sease #3, X1000.

Courtesy DuPont Laboratories, Parlin, N. J.

correct normal exposure. From this we can see that the Sease No. 3 formula is a developer which does not reduce all of the light-affected silver halide to metallic silver. The grain structure created by this developer, however, is very even and very satisfactory. The additional exposure required is very unsatisfactory because over-exposure with modern ultra-rapid panchromatic emulsions will result in poor tone quality. Whenever more than normal exposure is given an ultra-rapid emulsion, there will be a definite loss of quality in the highlights and throughout the whole tone range. This lack of quality is very real and it is a distinct disadvantage because it will eliminate that certain pearly lustre which should be a feature of a good print from a perfectly exposed and developed negative. The density of

43

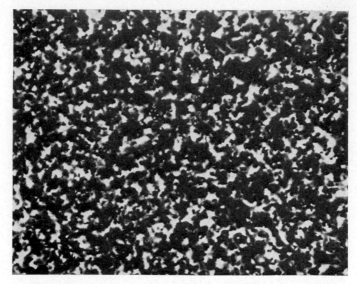

Photomicrograph of DuPont Superior film developed in D-76, X1000.

Courtesy DuPont Laboratories, Parlin, N. J.

negatives developed in the Sease #3 formula is very deceiving because the color imparted by the paraphenylenadiamine has a greater printing value than appears to the eye. For this reason negatives developed in a Sease #3 formula should appear to be much thinner or more delicate than negatives developed in the formula D-76-d.

The addition of metol to a paraphenyenediamine-glycin-sodium sulphite developer will greatly increase the film speed of that developer. The addition of the metol is, however, of doubtful value because there are certain disadvantages with the use of this chemical. The action of metol in this type of developer will be very similar to the action of metol when used with sodium sulphite alone. The silver grains in the emulsion will

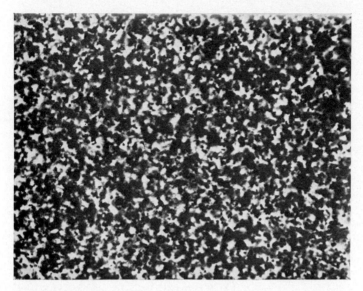

Photomicrograph of DuPont Superior film developed in Champlin #15, X1000. Note uniformity of grain structure.

Courtesy DuPont Laboratories, Parlin, N. J.

be shaved to a microscopic size. This shaving of the silver grains will leave large and irregular voids in between the grains and there will be a noticeable grain in the finished print. This action will, of course, be tempered somewhat with the paraphenylenediamine and glycin so that the effect of the grain structure will not be quite as coarse as if these chemicals were not present. Film speed will be increased by the metol. Negatives developed in a Sease #3 formula to which has been added two grams of metol per litre (30 grains: 32 ounces) will require 1.6 times the exposure necessary with the D-76-d developer. This difference in film speed is so slight as to be scarcely noticeable except in candid camera work. The action of this developer is splendid until the metol is exhausted. This dissipation of the metol cannot be accurately gauged and after it takes place, all of the good features of the combination are lost. Negatives will then lack proper tone gradation and shadow detail, while the highlights will be hard and almost unprintable.

A few years ago minicams were deluged with a lot of fine grain developers about which many extravagant claims were made. Every camera shop had its own pet developer put up in either a brown or blue bottle and a thriving business was done by those firms who put up their pet formula in cans. The salesman behind the counters led the man with the little camera to believe that the contents of this bottle or that particular can would solve all of his photographic problems. An analysis of all these developers showed that they were ordinary paraphenylenediamine-glycin developers to which had been added one, two, three, or four grams of metol per litre. The only real feature which the different manufacturers could possibly crow about was the fact that their developer contained more or less metol, although actually the secret formula of the developer was something never to be divulged. Not one of these manufacturers really offered anything except an unbelievable line of extravagant claims.

The only way to use a paraphenylenediamine-glycin-metol developer with any assurance of perfect, uniform results is to develop only one roll of film in it and then pour it down the sink. Too many fine grain developing specialists use this type of developer long after the metol is exhausted and this false economy of their's results in mile after mile of worthless negatives.

The results obtained from paraphenylenediamine-glycin-metol developers after a few rolls have passed through the solution gave rise to the belief that paraphenylenediamine should not be used as a developer. This belief has been pounced upon by the advocates of the metol-hydroquinone-borax wing of the miniature camera section of the photographic world and used as a basis for the condemnation of this chemical. Gentlemen all over the world have given their ideas and theories about just how the metol-hydroquinone-borax developer should be used and why it is so much better than paraphenylenediamine. All of this information advanced for our special benefit simmers down to the whole idea that a slight increase in exposure and a slight decrease in developing time will give very nice negatives with a comparatively fine grain. Actually, the grain size obtained by this method will be slightly less with fine grain films and slightly larger with ultra-rapid films, and is scarcely worth all the trouble involved. The greatest disadvantage to this continually proposed method of procedure is its effect upon high speed photography. Over-exposure and under-development of an ultra-rapid film emulsion will result in a flatness which no contrast printing paper can correct. Modern ultra-rapid emulsions require a minimum exposure and full development. There is no latitude in this respect. Then, too, over-exposure with ultra-rapid emulsions has a tendency to increase grain size somewhat because when light strikes a particle of silver salt in the emulsion, this light-affected silver particle infects all of the surrounding particles of silver salt. If we increase an exposure, we naturally increase this deflection of light so that more surrounding particles are affected. It follows then that in the process of development more silver grains will be whirled into little clumps and this agglomeration will naturally affect the finished print. Over-exposure, then, is to be avoided and any developer requiring more than a normal exposure is definitely not worth considering. It is, in fact, a hindrance to the advancement of miniature photography.

CHAPTER FIVE

Developing Developers

From the foregoing chapter it should be clear that the development of a miniature negative is a problem which can be divided into two parts: part one is a search for a fine and even grain structure, and part two is a search for a developer which will combine this fineness of grain structure with high emulsion speed.

Now, grain size is no problem because a straight paraphenylenediamine-sodium sulphite developer will reduce the silver halide to metallic silver without allowing troublesome agglomeration which results in a coarse grain structure. It is also possible to process negatives by the system advocated by Dr. Odell and known as physical development. Physical development consists of depositing silver upon the latent image formed by light in the silver salts in the emulsion. Physical development of negatives is nothing new and had been almost forgotten until revived by Dr. Odell. Results obtained by this process are very erratic and actually no finer grained than the structure created by a straight paraphenylenediamine - sodium sulphite developer. The problem confronting us is to combine this ultra-fine grain structure with normal emulsion speed.

Many claims have been made that this developer or that developer should be used for normal exposures.

"Kobe Twilight"   *H. Frederickson*

Developed in Champlin #5

"The modern photographer, amateur or professional, has so many perfected mechanical devices, different films, grades and kinds of papers and such varied fine grain developers with which to work that the thrill of experimenting need never cease in a lifetime. There is always a new effect to attain, a new combination to try, or a different technique to master. In short, photography today is an endless adventure."

—*Hansena Frederickson*

We should take as a standard of exposure time the Eastman formula D-76-d, compounded with metol, hydroquinone, sodium sulphite, and borax, because this developer will give a normal negative with an exposure calculated by a properly used photometer set in accordance with the film manufacturers' speed rating.

Tests have been made with most of the so-called normal exposure fine grain developing formulas in comparison with the density and shadow detail given by a properly used D-76 developer. The results were very interesting and showed that the normal exposure claims for these developers were somewhat exaggerated. Fine grain developing is comparatively new and so little is known about it that the average worker cannot standardize on a good fine grain normal speed developing formula because there does not seem to be any such formula.

Experiments were conducted in an effort to find a developer capable of giving negatives with both fine grain and high emulsion speed. This combination, of course, is the goal of all photographic chemists. These experiments, conducted by this writer and a group of friends, were first conducted upon all of the ordinary chemicals used in photography. These chemicals were combined with paraphenylenediamine and sulphite alone and with paraphenylenediamine, glycin, and sulphite. Experiments were made also with developers containing a high concentration of sodium sulphite and a small quantity of metol to which was added a little carbonate. The possibility of other mild alkalis than borax was investigated. These experiments showed that so far as fine grain was concerned, paraphenylenediamine was the supreme reducing agent.

The addition of sodium bisulphite gave slightly better shadow detail and extensive experiments were made with this chemical to determine whether or not it should be incorporated in the developer. Two grams per litre (1 grain per ounce) of sodium bisulphite showed a slight improvement in film speed, while ninety grams per litre had a marked restraining effect upon the dense portions of the negative, and this allowed prolonged development to bring out the weaker portions of the negative. The grain of negatives developed in a solution containing a high concentration of sodium bisul-

Arkell Burnap

Panatomic Filmpack, developed in Champlin #15

"*The average photographer, both amateur and professional, has heretofore had to combine with his ideas of pictorialism a certain amount of technical knowledge of chemistry and chemical reactions. The net result of this is that many a pictorialist is lost to the world because he goes off on a tangent of formulas and processing to such an extent that he loses sight of his real objective. This book of Mr. Champlin's is so thorough, so complete, and so detailed in information that one's mind is fully at rest regarding steps after the picture is on the film emulsion. We can spend all our time thinking of the picture we want with the full knowledge that the rest of the job is purely mechanical. For the first time I feel that now I can think of the picture and not the process.*" —*Arkell Burnap* phite was as fine as with a straight paraphenylenedia-mine-sodium sulphite developer, and while the film speed was increased to almost normal, this was a definite advance over the paraphenylenediamine-glycin developers to which was added some metol. The negatives had a much nicer brilliance with full detail in the shadows and a true velvety quality in the highlights, and were superior in tone value to a paraphenylenediamine-glycin-metol developer. The great disadvantage of the addition of sodium bisulphite was the instability of the solution. This developer, while giving much finer grained images and much more shadow detail than the so-called normal developers on the market at that time, was actually no more stable than those developers, and therefore not worth considering. One roll of film was sufficient to cause a heavy silver sludge to form upon the sides of the container, and this silver sludge naturally had a powerful influence upon the life of the developer. Tests with sodium bisulphite showed that acidifying paraphenylenediamine was really worth investigating.

The addition of other acids with more of a preserving action upon organic reducing chemicals was incorporated in a whole series of paraphenylenediamine-glycin-sodium sulphite developers. Lactic acid has often been used as a preservative of short lived organic reducing agents. This chemical has long been recommended as a preservative in amidol developers. Lactic acid was used in varying amounts with an ordinary Sease #3 formula. A slight improvement in the appearance of the developed image was noted. It was not enough of an improvement to warrant shouting about, but it did show that we were definitely upon the right track. Resorcin also was tried. This chemical is a phenol product and it exerted more of a preserving action upon the organic chemicals than did the lactic acid. The use of resorcin in fine grain developing solutions is by no means new; in fact, its use was advocated some years ago in combination with metol, hydroquinone, and borax. The formula was as follows:

Metol	15 grains	1 gram
Sodium Sulphite	1¾ ounces	50 grams
Hydroquinone	23 grains	1.5 grams
Resorcin	15 grains	1 gram
Sodium Borate (borax)	15 grains	1 gram
Water	20 ounces	625 ccs

Developing time: eight minutes at 65° Fahrenheit. The amount of resorcin recommended for use in any fine grain developer is one and one-half grams per litre (22 grains per 32 ounces).

A search into the possibilities of other benzine ring compounds led to salicylic acid. This chemical was incorporated in the developer in the amount of one gram per litre. Negatives developed in a solution containing a small amount of salicylic acid were far too dense and had too much contrast, indicating that there was a speeding up of the developing time. The developer was diluted with water and it was found that the same quantity of chemicals in an ordinary paraphenylenediamine-glycin developer could be diluted with as much as sixteen parts of water if salicylic acid were present in the developer. The preserving power of this chemical was then tremendous. In addition to this preserving power upon the organic reducing agents, salicylic acid had a marked softening effect upon the gelatin. Salicylic acid will soften almost anything and is, in fact, the basis of a great many corn cures. The softening effect upon gelatin is very similar to the effect of an alkali on gelatin in the process of development. If the gelatin is softened, the organic reducers will be able to penetrate easily and reduce all of the light-affected silver in the gelatin. The softening effect of salicylic acid was ideal because it really did a thorough job. It was a vast improvement over any of the alkalis usually recommended because it was actually a preserver and not a destroyer of the other chemicals in the solution. The great disadvantage of this chemical was the possibility that it might soften the gelatin too much and thereby cause serious reticulation. In the dilute form of the developer containing this chemical, this softening possibility was not so very great because there was not enough salicylic acid in the developer to cause much trouble unless the temperature was increased to 72° Fahrenheit.

Now, the temperature of any developer is of much more importance than is generally supposed. Metol is one chemical with much the same action regardless of temperature. Glycin, on the other hand, works best at temperatures about 70° Fahrenheit. Below 65° Fahrenheit, glycin becomes somewhat dormant, and below 62° Fahrenheit, its action ceases almost entirely. Paraphenylenediamine is another chemical working best at higher temperatures and is identical with glycin in this respect. At 73-74° Fahrenheit, both paraphenylenediamine and glycin are at their best, each exerting a maximum energy and working in perfect harmony.

The temperature of a dilute developer containing salicylic acid could not be raised to the very advantageous 73-74° Fahrenheit so that the glycin and paraphenylenediamine could work most efficiently because there was the ever present possibility of reticulation of the gelatin. This is a serious menace. If the temperature was maintained at about 70° Fahrenheit and the developer agitated continuously, perfect negatives would result. The addition of a small quantity of sodium bisulphite was found to be of some value in restraining the swelling effect of the gelatin. The formula used with these chemicals is as follows:

Champlin #5

Sodium Sulphite	¾	ounces	22.5	grams
Acid Salicylic	4	grains	.3	gram
Sodium Bisulphite	8	grains	.5	gram
Paraphenylenediamine	59	grains	4	grams
Glycin	59	grains	4	grams
Water	8	ounces	250	ccs

For use take one part of the above stock solution and fifteen parts of water. Developing time: thirty-five minutes at 73° Fahrenheit with continuous agitation.

The emulsion speed of this developer requires an exposure of 1.8 times that required for a D-76-d developer. The grain size is a little finer than that given by the

Sease #3 formula. This was an advance because emulsion speed had been increased from 2.8 times normal to 1.8 times normal without any sacrifice in the fineness of the grain structure. This developer was highly successful with those workers who realized that 70° Fahrenheit and continuous agitation really meant something and were instructions which had to be followed. The effect of this developer can truly be termed physico-chemical. There will be a noticeable silver precipitate. The breakdown of the developer is overcome completely by making a stock solution as above and diluting one ounce of the stock solution with fifteen ounces of water. This forms a working solution which is sufficient for one roll of film and will be enough for most of the miniature tanks on the market today. The working solution should be used only once and then discarded. The stock solution has been kept in a clear bottle and in a light room without any worry as to whether or not the stopper was on the bottle, and after two years there was no deterioration in the developing power of the solution. It is possible also to make this developer in powder form, mixing all of the ingredients together and then storing them in air-tight containers. There will be a slow fusion of all of the chemicals and in time there will be a breakdown of these chemicals due to this fusion and to oxidation.

It may be well to mention here that the practice of mixing chemicals together so that they will be aged en masse is really not a good one because most of the chemicals used in photography have their own particular work to do, and this work commences immediately when they are mixed in either the dry form or with water. Some manufacturers have made great claims about pre-aging but this practice is really not a good one.

The addition of a small quantity of metol to the #5 developer gave an increase to this developer's emulsion speed. The keeping qualities of the stock solution with the metol were very good. There was a considerable increase in grain size due to the presence of the metol.

The developer incorporating the metol was as follows:

Champlin #6

Sodium Sulphite	¾	ounce	22.5 grams
Acid Salicylic	4	grains	.3 gram
Sodium Bisulphite	8	grains	.5 gram
Paraphenylenediamine	59	grains	4 grams
Glycin	59	grains	4 grams
Water	8	ounces	250 ccs
Metol	15	grains	1 gram

For use, take one part of the above and fifteen parts of water. Developing time: thirty minutes at 70° Fahrenheit with continuous agitation. The grain structure of this developer will be more like the grain structure of an ordinary paraphenylenediamine-glycin-sodium sulphite developer to which has been added some metol. This, then, is no great advantage because the difference in emulsion speed is only the difference between 1.8 and 1.4 times normal. This difference is not enough of an advantage to compensate for the coarsening of the grain structure.

The amount of agitation given any negative during the process of development in any developer has a marked influence upon the developing time required for normal contrast. If the negatives are agitated continuously during the process of development, there will be as much as twenty per cent decrease in the time required to develop them to normal contrast. Moreover, there will be much less likelihood of streaks from the sprocket holes of 35 mm films and from the denser portions of all negatives when the developer is agitated continuously. These faults will likely occur when negatives are not agitated during development. Agitation will also rid the surface of the emulsion of any air-bells or bubbles which may form due to the release of air from the emulsion in solution. These bubbles prevent the developer from acting upon the film directly behind them, and when the film is fixed out, there might be little clear spots which will be unsightly in the finished print.

Salicylic acid was a valuable addition to the developer and a search was made for a companion chemical which

"Harbor Scene"   Harry Champlin

Contax; 85 mm. Triotar F:4; 1/100 sec. at F:16, with Zeiss 1.8x yellow-green filter; Agfa Superpan, developed in Champlin #7.

would counteract the softening effect of this chemical at temperatures around 73° Fahrenheit. Benzoic acid was tried and finally selected because this chemical too was of the benzine ring compounds and was, therefore, compatible with all the other phenol chemicals in the developer. Benzoic acid is, like salicylic acid, a preservative of phenol reducing agents and is, in addition, a restrainer of these reducing agents. The restraining action of benzoic acid is over the whole negative. It is not selective like potassium bromide which acts only upon the weaker deposits of the negative and one of the effects of this chemical is to delay or prolong development time. Chemical fog, which is usually present whenever highly concentrated sodium sulphite solutions are used, is reduced by benzoic acid.

When benzoic acid was added in very small quantities to the developing solution, it was found that the restraining power of this chemical prohibited very dilute solutions such as were allowed by formulas #5 and #6. It was also found that this chemical delayed swelling of the gelatin for a short period so that it was possible to develop films at the advantageous temperature of 73-74° Fahrenheit without the reticulation which might result if this chemical were not in the developer. The effect of any hardening agent in a developing solution is to delay swelling for a definite period and if the gelatin is left in water or developing solutions for longer than this period, the effect will wear off and swelling will take place. Benzoic acid delayed swelling for a period equal to the normal developing time of the solution. This action of the benzoic acid did not eliminate the need for a hardening bath after development was completed.

If more than one and one-half grams of benzoic acid is added to a litre of developer (22 grains per 32 ounces), the retarding or restraining effect of this chemical will be so great that the developing time will be prolonged beyond all reason and there is a possibility that reticulation might set in. This possibility arises from the fact that the prolongation of the developing time will be beyond the limits set by the hardening action of the benzoic acid and the gelatin structure will then be subject to the softening influence of the salicylic acid.

The benzoic acid made the sodium bisulphite superfluous and this last chemical was eliminated. This elimination of the sodium bisulphite was desirable principally because by leaving it out, we leave out one chemical which is not a member of the benzine ring and which has, therefore, nothing in common with the chemicals of that origin.

The addition of still another chemical was desirable because the balance between alkalinity and acidity of

Will Connell

Developed in Champlin #7

the solution was very delicate and had to be maintained. Boric acid is usually added to a developer when a buff r is required, and it is excellent for this purpose. The quantity of boric acid should be about two grams per litre (1 grain per ounce). If we increase the percentag of boric acid beyond certain limits, there will be a decided increase in the time required to develop a normal negative to correct contrast, and if the concentration of boric acid is too high, this chemical will act as a complete stop bath and no development will take place.

The presence of so many acids in the developer brought the alkalinity down to a pH of 7.15 or almost neutral. This was something different from the average photographic chemist's conception of a developer. The average photographic chemist will argue that when the alkalinity of a developer is lowered towards the neutral point, the emulsion speed of the developer will suffer. In bringing the alkalinity down to almost the neutral point of pH 7.0, there was an actual increase in the emulsion speed of the solution.

The concentration of paraphenylenediamine and glycin was higher than is usually recommended in fine grain developing. Tests showed that these two reducing agents and the acids and other chemicals gave negatives with a certain lack of shadow detail which meant that the negatives were not fully balanced. The addition of either metol or amidol was deemed necessary in order that full shadow detail could be recorded in the process of the reduction of silver halide to metallic silver. Amidol was far superior for the purpose, but it is a chemical with a very short life when dissolved in the presence of sodium sulphite. Metol is probably more satisfactory for general use because it will have a long life, and just enough metol must be added to do the work required and no more. About two grams of metol per litre (1 grain per ounce) should be added. The developer should be made up as follows:

Champlin #7

Water	20	ounces	1000	ccs
Metol	25	grains	2.5	grams
Sodium Sulphite	1	ounce	45	grams
Acid Benzoic	9	grains	1	gram
Acid Salicylic	4	grains	0.5	gram
Acid Boric	25	grains	2.5	grams
Glycin	¼	ounce	11.5	grams
Paraphenylenediamine	¼	ounce	11.5	grams

This developer should be used at full strength and the first roll should be developed at 70° Fahrenheit. The second roll should be developed at 73° Fahrenheit and each succeeding roll requires an additional two minutes developing time for full contrast. Developing time for

Eastman Super-X and DuPont Superior 35 mm films is nineteen and one-half minutes.*

The first roll developed will have considerably more grain than will subsequent rolls. This is because the metol and the other chemicals in this solution are in their strongest state and create a tremendous turbulence within the emulsion in the process of development. This effect is tempered by the first roll of film developed in the solution and all other rolls will have a slightly better and more delicate tonal range. Some workers have advocated a reduction of about twenty per cent in the developing time for the first roll and claim that this reduction will eliminate these differences in grain size. Tests have proved that the developing time given for this formula are correct. Other workers have exposed a roll of film to light and then dropped it in the developer to temper it. This practice is not worthwhile as the grain size is still small enough and is, in fact, smaller than that given by the average fine grain developer.

There is an idea existing in the minds of some workers that the incorporation of silver in the developer will improve that developer. This practice is to be strongly discouraged because silver in a developer causes a real breakdown of the chemicals in that developer. Pure silver nitrate is not the same as the double silver bromide salt which is dissolved out of the developer. This silver bromide salt is a combination of silver nitrate and either potassium or ammonium bromide. These two chemicals when mixed, form a precipitate and this precipitate is the silver bromide which is the light-sensitive silver salt in the emulsion. If you add bromide to any developer, there will be a restraining effect upon the weaker portions of the negative. This restraining effect will surely result in a loss of shadow detail. This loss of shadow detail is a very serious matter with paraphenylenediamine-glycin-sulphite developers and can com-

---

*Developing times for a full list of films are given in Appendixes A and B.

pletely counteract the effect of the addition of metol to the developer. If you take a freshly mixed para-phenylenediamine - glycin - sulphite developer and drop into it a few crystals of silver nitrate, you will see that these silver nitrate crystals are immediately converted to a fine black sediment which will sink at once to the bottom of the bottle. The reducing agents have seized upon the silver nitrate and have converted it to metallic silver. In so doing, the reducing agents have exerted a certain proportion of their potential strength upon it. The silver nitrate is an oxidizing agent and the developer is a reducing agent. All that happens is that silver metal is formed and the developer is used up. The developer is now no longer as strong nor does it have the reduction potential as when freshly mixed. For this reason, silver loading, sometimes termed pre-ageing and sometimes given other fanciful terms, is of doubtful value.

Negatives developed in formula #7 will show a vast improvement in film speed over the so-called normal exposure fine grain developers; in fact, this developer can be used for exposures for from one-half to a full stop less than usually called for by modern film emulsions. Modern high speed lenses and ultra-rapid film emulsions can be used to fullest advantage with this developer, and while the formula is not intended as the ultimate in developers, it is a distinct advance over any of the formulas published prior to its appearance in CAMERA CRAFT in August, 1936.

The amount of sodium sulphite in this developer is less than is usually recommended with paraphenylene-diamine. This was found by actual tests to give additional emulsion speed and is one of the reasons why this formula #7 had more emulsion speed than other developers. Sodium sulphite is necessary in a developer because it is a preservative of the reducing agents in that developer. Its action is to oxidize to sodium sulphate and in so doing, to preserve the organic substances from attack by oxygen in the water and air. Now, if the con-

"James Guthrie"   *Paul Dorsey*
          Courtesy Time, Inc., and Life

Contax; 50 mm. Sonnar F:1.5; developed in Champlin #9.

"The Champlin #15 formula fills a long felt need in newspaper work."

—*Paul Dorsey*

centration of sodium sulphite is too high, so much oxygen will be absorbed by this process that there will be little left for the reducing agents and developing time will be prolonged. Most of the fine grain formulas offered to the miniature camera world contain entirely too much sodium sulphite, and this fact accounts for the increase in exposure time necessary to secure perfectly graded negatives. This fact also accounts for the prolonged development time of most fine grain developers. The increase in exposure time is necessitated by the solvent action of the sodium sulphite upon the silver in the emulsion. The more sulphite there is in the developer, the more silver there will be dissolved out of the film emulsion, and this loading of the developer with silver will cause a natural breakdown of the developer, resulting in a loss of reducing power.

The average fine grain formula calls for from ninety to one hundred grams of sodium sulphite per litre of developer (3-3½ ounces per 32 ounces). A reduction to one-half of this amount will result in a definite increase in emulsion speed. This is true with almost all of the fine grain formulas which have been brought out during the past ten years. The high concentration of paraphenylenediamine and glycin in formula #7 is far above the average, and this, too, results in a greater reduction of light-affected silver halide to metallic silver. Indeed, this action is greater than that of almost any other developer. The emulsion speed of formula #7 can only be realized if the temperature is at 70° Fahrenheit or higher. Below this temperature the paraphenylenediamine and glycin become somewhat dormant, whereas at 62° Fahrenheit these chemicals almost cease to function. At the higher temperatures all of the components of the developer are exerting a maximum energy and efficiency, and this, too, accounts for the high emulsion speed of this developer.

The success of formula #7 spurred on the work of experimentation, and the ideas incorporated in that developer were used as a basis from which to work.

Formula #7 contains a small quantity of metol. The metol was used to give a small margin of shadow detail and this is as it should be. However, metol and paraphenylenediamine are not a compatible pair of chemicals for fine grain work. Metol is a very energetic reducing agent. Paraphenylenediamine is slow working and so mild that the grain structure of the negative is not greatly affected. Glycin is a buffer and is used to take care of the paraphenylenediamine. Metol, when combined with paraphenylenediamine, still retains its energy and has a tendency to upset the fine grain work done by the paraphenylenediamine. Metol is therefore somewhat of a necessary evil and its elimination was greatly desired. A substitute for metol was sought.

Pyrogallic acid is a reducing agent with a reduction potential as great as that of metol; in other words, metol can be counted upon to reduce a maximum amount of silver halide to metallic silver and pyro has this same characteristic. Pyro will give much greater delicacy in the separation of tones. A reducing agent with a maximum reduction ability is absolutely necessary if correct shadow detail is to be obtained in a negative.

This can be produced in a negative if we are willing to sacrifice fine grain. Developers containing metol, hydroquinone, sodium sulphite, and borax will give full shadow detail but the grain size will be far too large. Formula #7 will also give full shadow detail and the grain size will be very satisfactory. Ordinary formulas containing paraphenylenediamine, glycin, sodium sulphite and metol will require about 1.4 times normal exposure and will give a slightly coarser grain size. The grain structure of formula #7 will not be as fine as the grain structure of a negative developed in a straight paraphenylenediamine-sodium sulphite developer or in the #5 formula, although it is actually better than that produced by most of the fine grain formulas offered today. A Paraphenylenediamine-sodium sulphite developer, while giving extremely fine grain, cannot really be considered because the additional exposure required with this developer is beyond reason. Fine grain and high emulsion speed can be combined in one developer. This fact was definitely proved by formula #7 because with this developer emulsion speed could actually be increased over the manufacturers' recommendations. The grain structure was a decided improvement over the grain structure created by the sodium sulphite-borax type of developers. It was an improvement also over the paraphenylenediamine-glycin-sodium sulphite-metol developers. This formula was something new both in composition and recommended temperature. It was new also in the fact that it ignored the old idea that high alkalinity and high emulsion speed went hand in hand. The metol in the developer was the one chemical capable of producing an upset in the fine grain structure and this fact accounts for the experiments with pyro.

The image given by metol is a neutral gray-black. The image given by pyrogallic acid is more of a yellow-ish-black because there is a certain amount of yellow stain in a pyro developed negative. The actual amount of yellow stain in a pyro developed negative is in inverse proportion to the amount of sodium sulphite in the developer. In other words, if the sodium sulphite concentration in a pyro developer is low, the resulting stain will be very heavy, whereas if the concentration of sodium sulphite is high, there will be very little stain. This stain-giving property of pyro was one of its prime assets in the early days of photography because the stain gave a print with a perfect range of tones from black to white. For those unfamiliar with the action of pyro, it may be well to explain that the stain is in direct proportion to the amount of light-affected silver in the emulsion, being heaviest in the dense portions and graduating down to an almost colorless deposit in the finest portions of the negative. Some years ago pyro advocates used this developer with a very small quantity of sodium sulphite. This practice gave a yellowish

Harry Champlin

Contax; 85 mm. Sonnar F:2; 1/50th sec. at F:16, on Agfa Superpan; developed in Champlin #9.

stained image in place of the ordinary black image which we are accustomed to see in a negative. This stain had an excellent printing value with a far longer tone scale than is usual with other reducing agents. The actual metallic silver image was then bleached out, leaving nothing but the stained image, and since the stain had a comparatively small grain structure, the resulting image was delicate and exceedingly fine. This practice was excellent but it had one fault—the stain was almost impossible to control. Then, too, the stained image was too delicate and had to be projected onto a contrast paper. Modern high sulphite content developers prevent the heavy stain which is the outstanding feature of a pyro developer. There is some stain, however, when pyro is used in the developer and this fact led to a series of experiments with this chemical. The metol was eliminated from the #7 formula and a like amount of pyro substituted for it. To make up for the large quantity of sulphite in the solution, it was necessary to increase the pyro because a normal quantity had practically no effect. The amount of pyro was increased to the extent that the sodium sulphite-pyro balance was about the same as the balance in an ordinary low sulphite pyro developer. A developer of this composition was as follows:

Champlin #8

Sodium Sulphite	3½	ounces	100 grams
Pyro	¾	ounce	34.5 grams
Acid Benzoic	36	grains	2.4 grams
Acid Salicylic	15	grains	1 gram
Acid Boric	75	grains	7.5 grams
Glycin	¾	ounce	34.5 grams
Paraphenylenediamine	¾	ounce	34.5 grams
Water	64	ounces	2 litres

This developer had a tendency to frill the edges of the negatives at 73-74° Fahrenheit. This temperature was found by test to be the most desirable because it gave nicely stained images with full emulsion speed and a very satisfactory grain structure. Because of the tendency towards too much softening of the gelatin, it was deemed advisable to incorporate a more drastic hardener than one giving the effect produced by the benzoic acid. Sodium sulphate was selected as a hardener because this chemical is inert photographically and will not change or affect the action of the other chemicals in the developer. The amount of sodium sulphate added to the formula #8 was fifty grams per litre (1½ ounces per 32 ounces) of the anhydrous form of the chemical. The effect of the sodium sulphate was to delay swelling of the gelatin for a period considerably longer than that of the benzoic acid.

With all of these chemicals in the solution, it became necessary to add still another to keep them in solution. The most suitable chemical for this purpose was an alcohol. Many alcohols were tried and many were found suitable, but iso propyl alcohol 97% was selected because of its ability to dissolve almost anything. It does smell to high heaven, but it does do a thorough job, and it will keep the chemicals in solution. In fact, this developer will keep the anti-halation gray coatings of gray back 35 mm films in solution after they have been dissolved out of the emulsion. The developer with these two additions was as follows:

Champlin #10

Sodium Sulphite	3½ ounces	100	grams
Pyro	¾ ounce	34.5	grams
Acid Benzoic	36 grains	2.4	grams
Acid Salicylic	15 grains	1	gram
Acid Boric	75 grains	7.5	grams
Glycin	¾ ounce	34.5	grams
Paraphenylenediamine	¾ ounce	34.5	grams
Water	64 ounces	2	litres
Alcohol Iso Propyl 97%	3 ounces	90	ccs
Sodium Sulphate	3½ ounces	100	grams

This developer has exceptional keeping qualities, improves with use, and will develop more film per litre than most any other fine grain developer. The improvement with use is due directly to the fact that the pyro in the developer deteriorates rapidly, forming a heavily stained solution. With this deterioration the stain producing effect upon the film will increase. There is then more of a stained image after the developer has been used for some time than when it was first freshly mixed. Tests have shown that each gallon of this developer will develop about eighty-five rolls of film and for this reason it is an excellent tank developer for regular fine grain finishing work.

The grain structure of a negative developed in a freshly mixed formula #10 will not be quite as fine as the grain structure of a negative developed in formula #7. This is due to the fact that pyro is, like metol, an energetic reducing agent. There is some turbulence in the emulsion during the process of development. The high concentration of pyro is necessary for a proper stain, and this naturally results in some increase in agglomeration or bunching of the silver grains. The turbulence created by pyro is lessened as the developer is used, and with each succeeding roll there is an increase in the yellow stain.

The most satisfactory results in fine grain work cannot be attained with pyrogallic acid as a part of the developer. This chemical, like metol, was too much of a disturbing factor and created too much of a turbulence during the process of development. A low concentration of pyro would have been perfectly satisfactory if the staining properties of this chemical could be retained in a highly concentrated sodium sulphite solution. This, of course, was a difficulty because an increase in sulphite would naturally result in a decrease of the yellow stain given by the pyrogallic acid. Experiments were conducted with pyro derivatives. Rubinol, a Defender product, gave some very satisfactory results in the tests made with it. This substance had all of the good features of pyro and lacked many of pyro's disadvantages for fine grain work. Rubinol can be used with sodium sulphite and will give very nice images without the addition of any other chemical. In combination with paraphenylenediamine it forms a fair fine grain developer. The grain structure of images developed in paraphenylenediamine-rubinol-sodium sulphite are not as fine as formula #7 and are only slightly finer that formula D-76-d. Rubinol can be used in highly concentrated sodium sulphite solutions without impairing its stain-giving qualities. The quantity of rubinol used to replace the metol in formula #7 was three and one-half grams per litre. Any more than this amount will allow the rubinol to do actual reducing of the silver halide to metallic silver. If this reduction by the rubinol actually takes place, there will be much more grain in the negative than is desired in fine grain work. The amount of rubinol should, therefore, be just sufficient to create a slight stain upon the latent image without actually reducing much of the silver halide to metallic silver. Another feature noted with the addition of rubinol to the formula #7 was that this chemical seemed to energize the process of development so that the actual developing time for a given contrast was less than that required by formula #7. This decrease in time was about twenty per cent of the times given for formula #7. The negatives developed in the test solutions containing two and one-half grams of rubinol per litre and no metol had a coarser grain structure than negatives developed in formula #7. This was a disadvantage.

A series of extensive tests showed that still another chemical was needed if pyro or any of its derivatives was to be used in fine grain work. The chemical selected for this purpose was digallic acid (tannic acid), and this made the rubinol a much better addition to the developer than metol. Tannic acid can be used with other chemicals as a mordant in the dye process. In this process a relief image is created from the latent image formed by light in the emulsion. The gelatin is chemically hardened in direct proportion to the amount of light-affected silver salts in the emulsion. If this relief image is bathed with certain dyes or with certain other chemicals, a real image will be formed because the dyes or other chemicals used will adhere strongly to the dense portions of the image and weakly to the finer portions of the image and not at all to those parts which were unaffected by light.

Now, something of this sort happens when tannic acid and rubinol are incorporated in the #7 developer. The image created by the reduction process and by the staining process was of a yellowish green color. This yellowish green color was almost transparent to the eye and yet it had a very strong restraining effect upon light in the enlarger. For this reason the images are very fine and delicate and still give stronger prints than denser appearing negatives developed, for example, in formula D-76-d. This is a decided advantage because miniature negatives should have a certain delicacy of tone values. They have to be enlarged to many times their original size, and if the separation of tones in the negative is too strong, the resulting enlargements allow far too much contrast. Herein lies the true secret of success in miniature camera work. The tone scale of the negative should be such as to make a poor contact print because the delicacy of the tone values is too fine and does not appear to advantage in a contact print. The most delicate separation of tone values will be intensified in the enlarging process.

Tannic acid had a restraining effect upon rubinol so that developing times were the same as for the formula #7. Iso propyl alcohol 97% was added because the high chemical content of the developer could have easily created a precipitate in cold weather. The developer using this combination of chemicals was as follows:

Champlin #9

Water	20	ounces	1000	ccs
Rubinol (Defender)	32	grains	3.5	grams
Sodium Sulphite	1½	ounces	60	grams
Acid Benzoic	18	grains	2	grams
Acid Salicylic	4	grains	0.5	gram
Acid Boric	25	grains	2.5	grams
Acid Digallic (Tannic)	9	grains	1	gram
Glycin	¼	ounce	11.5	grams
Paraphenylenediamine	¼	ounce	11.5	grams
Alcohol Iso Propyl 97%	1	ounce	50	ccs

The developing time with this formula should be

"*Windows*"   *Rowena Rathbone*

Agfa Superpan, exposed at Weston 40; developed in Champlin #9.

"Modern photography with its boldness, accuracy of detail, and various uses such as photomurals and posters, demands the kind of fine grain developer produced by Harry Champlin, for in no other way can grainless enlargements be made as large as desired, and as often as desired."

                                        —*Rowena Rathbone*

based upon the length of time required to secure a nice stained image. If the developing time is prolonged beyond this time, the image will become blacker, showing that the rubinol is doing its share of the reducing process, and there will be a coarsening of the grain structure of the negative. The yellowish green stain produced by this developer will have a far greater printing value and show a much finer separation of tone values than will a correctly developed D-76-d negative. The yellowish green stain is responsible also for the high emulsion speed of this developer. It seems that the stain of rubinol is more effective upon the shadowed portions of the negative than the ordinary type of reducing agents. The stain will act perfectly and within a relatively short time upon shadow detail; in fact, the stained shadow detail will be stronger in proportion to the highlights than the ordinary shadow-highlight brilliance of an ordinary negative. Care must be exercised, however, that these negatives are not over-developed because if they are over-developed, there will be a blackening of the image and contrast will be built up. This blackening of the image will also cause a coarsening of the grain structure. Negatives over-developed in the #9 formula will have a coarser grain structure than negatives developed in D-76-d. With the #9 formula, like with all of the formulas in this series, the temperature should be around 70-72° Fahrenheit.

Formula #9 was just as much of a success with the miniature camera enthusiasts as was formula #7. We were deluged with letters from all over the country, letters from amateurs who had used these formulas and were enthusiastic about them. Formula #9 created the same controversy among chemists as formula #7. Regardless of their statements and paper calculations, the fact remained that these two formulas actually did a better job of fine grain developing.

Experiments have shown that everything is not known about the chemistry of photography, and this probably accounts for the merry-go-round of ideas, ideas which usually end up with the same formulas, the same chemicals, and the same results. Photography is truly a science of the highest order and it is in its infancy. For this reason we cannot condemn a developer or any new method of producing an image upon film just because it is not in accordance with the ideas of recognized photographic chemists. Formulas #7 and #9 were new and accomplished more than the other fine grain formulas offered. They were by no means the ultimate in developers.

So little is known about the image formed by light upon the sensitive silver in the film that there are possibilities of entirely new trends in the treatment of this subject. Some authorities believe that the latent image is chemical, while other authorities believe that it is purely physical. The actual attraction of one silver particle to another has not been definitely determined. No one can actually say what takes place in the dark in a developing solution. The theory uppermost today is that the alkalinity of a developer causes a breakdown of the gelatin and results in an explosion of the silver halide when attacked by the reducing agents. This theory is the commonly accepted one. The explosion, it seems, is the cause of the agglomeration or bunching or clumping of the silver grains. The theory also reasons that the higher the alkalinity or pH of the developer, the more reduction of silver halide to metallic silver there will be. This theory does not account for the fact that in formulas #7 and #9 the alkalinity is reduced to almost neutral and yet there was no sacrifice in emulsion speed or grain size; in fact, there was an enhanced emulsion speed due to a reduction in the alkalinity of these developing formulas.

Experiments along an entirely different line of thought have proved to be intensely interesting. In any emulsification there is a certain dormant static potential. The process of development places the silver salts in a solution which has a tendency to release this potential. The silver grains are attracted to one another as if by a magnetic force. If this theory of ours is true, it would seem most logical that any means which might restrain this magnetic impulse would naturally prevent a certain amount of the agglomeration or clumping which takes place during the process of development. This theory is not an original one because some one tried years ago to solve such a problem by using electrodes in the developing tank but this was not the correct way to attack the problem. It did not accomplish anything.

The addition of some metal to the developer might be a far better way to attack this problem. If some metallic salt was added to the developer, the silver in the emulsion might become a non-conductor, and therefore might not be affected by any magnetic force. This, then, is the basis for a long series of experiments. Now, the natural metal to incorporate in the developer in order to accomplish this purpose was nickel. In the manufacture of stainless steels which are non-magnetic, nickel and chromium are used. Nickel is the basis of Monel-metal. The addition of nickel in the metallic form to other metals creates a metal which is a non-conductor. In photographic chemistry we must naturally use nickel salts. These are obtainable as chlorides and sulphates.

Nickel chloride crystals were powdered and then dissolved in a small quantity of water. Two grams of nickel chloride in about thirty ccs of distilled water were added to one litre of the formula #9. The developer clouded immediately, changing to an olive green color. A precipitate formed which took about twenty-four hours to settle to the bottom of the beaker. The solution was then filtered and the clear liquid filtrate was used as a developer. The negatives produced by this developer were the finest in appearance, printing quality, and emulsion speed of any which this writer has ever seen. The grain structure was finer than that produced by formula #7 and the shadow detail indicated a high emulsion speed. The life of the developer was short, indicating that the nickel had had a very serious

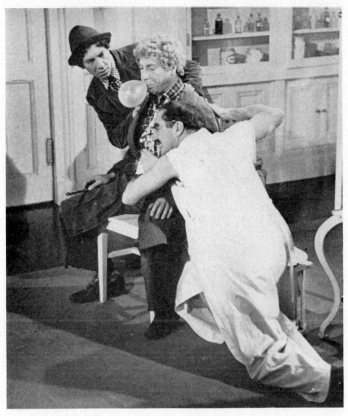

The Marx Brothers playing in M.G.M.'s "Day At The Races".
Courtesy Time, Inc., and Life.

Developed in Champlin #15.

effect upon the organic substances in the solution. The precipitate filtered out of this developer was mainly tannic acid and there was, of course, a certain amount of the surplus of the other chemicals in the solution which, too, were dissolved out.

A long series of experimental developers were then

made, each one eliminating one chemical of the formula #9 and each one including nickel chloride in the amount of two grams per litre of developer. This was, of course, an experiment by trial and error because trial and error is actually the best method of determining anything. It may be longer, but it is surer. Tannic acid was found to be the greatest offender and this chemical refused to dissolve in the presence of the nickel chloride. A developer was made up with all of the ingredients of the formula #9 except the tannic acid, and experiments were conducted with it. The results obtained from the original solution containing nickel chloride were vastly superior to a developer containing no tannic acid. Moreover, it was possible to duplicate the results of the first nickel chloride developer time and again. This proved that the addition of the metal was really worth while. This was indeed interesting.

An attempt was made to replace the acidity of the tannic acid which precipitated out when nickel was added. Hydrochloric acid was used for this purpose. The hydrochloric acid naturally brought the pH or acid-alkalinity down to the same level as did the tannic acid. There was actually no decrease in developing power of the solution when hydrochloric acid was added, although there was a considerable increase in the coarseness of the grain structure of the emulsion. Here again was proof positive that the lowering of the alkalinity of the developer did not necessarily mean that emulsion speed of that developer was decreased. The developer using nickel chloride was as follows:

Champlin #11

Water	20	ounces	1000	ccs
Rubinol (Defender)	32	grains	3.5	grams
Sodium Sulphite	1½	ounces	60	grams
Acid Benzoic	18	grains	2	grams
Acid Salicylic	4	grains	0.5	gram
Acid Boric	25	grains	2.5	grams
Acid Digallic	9	grains	1	gram
Glycin	¼	ounce	11.5	grams
Paraphenylenediamine	¼	ounce	11.5	grams
Alcohol Iso Propyl 97%	1	ounce	50	ccs
Nickel Chloride	20	grains	2	grams

Charles Kerlee

DuPont Superior film developed in Champlin #15.

Dissolve the chemicals in the order given. If crystaline or technical paraphenylenediamine is used, this should be heated to 180° Fahrenheit in a small quantity of water and added to the solution. The nickel chloride should not be added until the developer is cooled to 70° Fahrenheit. There will be a cloudiness which will turn to a thick precipitate with much the same appearance as pea soup. This precipitate should be allowed to settle and then filtered off, after which the developer will be ready for use. The life of this developer is very short, depending upon the amount of film developed in it.

The reaction between the nickel chloride, paraphenylenediamine, glycin, and tannic acid was really not a desirable one. The results obtained by the addition of nickel chloride to the developer were so revolutionary as far as emulsion speed, grain structure, and tone quality were concerned, that experiments were continued with the other salt forms of this chemical. Nickel sulphate was added to the developer in the same amount of two grams per litre. The reaction was much the same. There was the same precipitate which had to be filtered out and the same olive green colored solution after filtering. The developing time was increased over that required by the nickel chloride, and there was also a slightly coarser grain structure. This coarsening of the grain structure was due to the fact that to build up a given density of image required a much longer immersion of the film in the solution, and this longer immersion gave a much greater agglomeration or clumping of the silver grains. It appears that films can only be left in these new type solutions for a definite period without coarsening the grain structure.

This brings up the old idea that any attempt to produce a given gamma or contrast of a film will result in the same graininess or coarseness of the grain structure regardless of the developer used. This idea has been exploded time and again, but it seems that some people

"We Point With Pride"   *Harry Champlin*

Contax; 85 mm. Triotar F:4; DuPont Superior exposed at Weston 64; developed in Champlin #15. Notice that with the high emulsion speed rating of Weston 64, full shadow detail has been obtained in the telegraph pole and the buildings in the middle distance, and that aerial perspective and highlight gradation are well maintained.

still believe that such is actually the case. The grain structure is a result of the action of the chemicals in the developer and has nothing whatsoever to do with a standard gamma or contrast. It is true, however, that if films are left in a developer for longer than is necessary to produce correct contrast, there will be a natural coarsening of the grain structure.

One feature was noted in developers made with either nickel chloride or nickel sulphate, and that was the tremendous amount of shadow detail given by these developers in proportion to the highlight detail. In fact, it was possible to develop a negative of a scene with great contrast and to balance this negative perfectly in the developer. The shadow detail would be built up long before it was possible to attain maximum density in the highlights. This was a feature not to be found in any other high emulsion speed developer, fine grain or otherwise. This shadow-density property of the developer was somewhat the same so far as shadow detail was concerned as the practice of over-exposing and under-developing followed by so many miniature camera workers. The main difference, however, was in the brilliance and sparkle to the highlights of a print from a negative developed in a formula containing a nickel salt.

Another feature peculiar to this developer is that the visual and printing densities are far different. No color is apparent to the eye, and yet the printing time required for a negative which appears to have no more than average density will be at least twice that required for a properly exposed and developed D-76-d negative of the same apparent density. This feature will be at once apparent to any one making an enlargement from a negative developed in the #11 formula. The color is not the same as the yellow green stain of the #9 formula.

Still another feature peculiar to this developer is that the paraphenylenediamine stain is not quite so great.

Harry E. Crawford

Contax; 50 mm. Sonnar F:1.5; Super X, exposed at Weston 64, developed in Champlin #15.

"I find that with a minimum exposure and slight variation in developing time, I can get any contrast desired without fog, and can snap out pictures with great carrying quality."

—Harry E. Crawford

The paraphenylenediamine stain will certainly assert itself if any of the solution is spilled and allowed to dry and oxidize upon any surface. Paraphenylenediamine requires an extraordinary amount of care in use if stains are to be prevented. The best way for the amateur photographer to handle a tankful of developer containing this chemical is to place the tank in a tray or any other receptacle and to shake the receptacle and not handle the tank or allow any of the contents to spill out of the receptacle during the process of development. If any developer is spilled, it should be wiped up immediately and the place washed with soap and water. This will save repainting the kitchen. The hands should be washed with a mild alkaline soap such as that made by the Pacific Coast Borax Company and sold under the trade name 'Boraxo.'

Extensive experiments by Harry Crawford with the #11 formula showed that this developer improved with age and at the end of thirty days all of the ingredients in the developer were working harmoniously. There was no loss in emulsion speed, and the grain structure was finer than when first mixed. The keeping qualities of this developer were excellent regardless of the conditions under which it was kept. Neither brown nor blue bottles were required, and it was not necessary to keep the bottles in a dark room or closet. The used solution clouded rapidly and in some instances actually plated the container with a coating of pure silver. This plating was actually heavy enough to transform the beakers into mirrors. This was specially true if the developer contained nickel chloride and was not quite so pronounced when nickel sulphate was used.

In electro plating, nickel and ammonium sulphate are sometimes used. This double salt was tried and it had very much the same characteristics as the nickel chloride in the developer. The amount of nickel and ammonium sulphate first used was two grams per litre and a developer was made using this chemical as follows:

Philip M. Chancellor

Leica; 90 mm. Thambar; Super X, exposed at Weston 32, by Mazda
light; developed in Champlin #15.

*"In photography, art and science go hand in hand. The develop-
ment of a negative is just as important as the composition of the
picture."*

—*Philip M. Chancellor*

Champlin #14

Water	20	ounces	1000 ccs
Rubinol or Pyro	32	grains	3.5 grams
Sodium Sulphite	1½	ounces	60 grams
Acid Benzoic	12	grains	1.2 grams
Acid Salicylic	4	grains	0.5 grams
Acid Boric	25	grains	2.5 grams
Acid Digallic (Tannic)	9	grains	1 gram
Glycin	¼	ounce	11.5 grams
Paraphenylenediamine	¼	ounce	11.5 grams
Alcohol Iso Propyl 97%	1	ounce	50 ccs
Nickel & Ammonium Sulphate	20	grains	2 grams

The amount of nickel and ammonium sulphate was decreased in test developer #15 to ten grains (1 gram). The addition of the double salt of nickel and ammonium sulphate was better than either nickel chloride or nickel sulphate. Developing time was decreased quite a lot and the grain structure was finer. There was no sacrifice in the tremendous emulsion speed noticed in the first trial with nickel salts in the developer. This developer works splendidly at 68° Fahrenheit, giving negatives with a pleasing warm tone which denote the same deceptive printing values as noted in formula #11. The formula was then as follows:

Champlin #15 Formula

Water	20	ounces	1000 ccs
Rubinol or Pyro	32	grains	3.5 grams
Sodium Sulphite	1½	ounces	60 grams
Acid Benzoic	12	grains	1.2 grams
Acid Salicylic	4	grains	0.5 grams
Acid Boric	25	grains	2.5 grams
Acid Digallic (Tannic)	9	grains	1 gram
Glycin	¼	ounce	11.5 grams
Paraphenylenediamine	¼	ounce	11.5 grams
Alcohol Iso Propyl 97%	1	ounce	50 ccs
Nickel & Ammonium Sulphate	10	grains	1 gram

In compounding the #15 formula, the chemicals should be mixed in the order shown. Paraphenylenediamine should be mixed separately in a small quantity of water which has been heated to about 180° Fahrenheit. After this has been added to the developer and the solution has been cooled to 70° Fahrenheit, dissolve the nickel and ammonium sulphate in a small quantity of water (1 ounce) and add very slowly to the developer. A precipitate may form at the top of the container and slowly settle to the bottom. If the precipitate forms and settles, the developer should be filtered. If no precipitate forms, the developer should be filtered nevertheless. *This filtering is important and failure will result if it is not carefully carried out.*

This developer has been mixed and bottled and presented to at least one hundred well known miniature camera photographers. Negatives have been developed in it for Time and Life magazines, for newspapers all over the country, and for motion picture studios, and these negatives are as nearly perfect as it is possible to make a negative with the knowledge of today. Amateur photographers who do not know much about developing film can take this developer and make better negatives than they have ever made before. There will be shadow detail such as has never been present in negatives before. There will be brilliant highlights without the blocking up or terrific contrast given by so many paraphenylenediamine - sulphite- metol formulas. The grain structure will be fine enough for eleven by fourteen glossy enlargements from ultra-rapid films such as DuPont Superior and Eastman Super-X. The keeping qualities of this developer are excellent. Each thirty-two ounces of developer will develop ten rolls of film. These ten rolls of film will be correctly developed. This formula has been used in the writer's laboratory for thousands of rolls of 35 mm miniature camera film. Some of this film was for major motion picture studios, some for universities, and some for travelers. These films could not be duplicated. The developer never once failed to give perfect negatives. This can not be said of any other fine grain developing formula. The reader of this book is strongly urged to try this formula because if he does try it, he will adopt it for all of his negatives.

In addition to the perfect gradation and fine grain qualities, this developer will permit shooting at unbe-

Developed in Champlin #15.

From a 53 times linear enlargement of the picture which appears on the facing page. Relative size of the contact print is shown in the lower left corner, with the area enlarged outlined in black.

lievable speeds. DuPont Superior and Eastman Super-X films can be exposed in daylight at 64 Weston and under artificial light at 24 to 32 Weston. This is practically impossible with any other developer. This emulsion speed of formula #15 will save many negatives which might otherwise be ruined through under-exposure.

All of the formulas known to miniature photography have been experimented with by this writer and a group of friends in an attempt to solve the problem confronting us. This problem, as has been stated many times in this book, concerns high emulsion speed and fine grain in one developer. So far as this writer is concerned, the problem has been solved by the formula #15.

The formulas printed in this book are new and are not just a rehash of what has been said time and again for the past ten years. There is no mystery to them; there are no cards up anyone's sleeve. This book has been written so that the miniature camera workers will understand something about development and the chemicals used in fine grain work. The only way to advance is through the knowledge of many people. Only by an exchange of ideas can we hope to advance. There is no claim that any formula in this book is the ultimate in fine grain developers. There is a claim that the formula #15 is better than any other developer on the market at the present time. If this formula or any of the ideas incorporated in this book will help anyone to produce a better developer, the book will have served its purpose.

CHAPTER SIX

Causes of Failure

There has been a deluge of letters from all over the world in which there were questions concerning the processing of films. Some letters were from amateurs who had read this writer's articles on fine grain development in CAMERA CRAFT and wanted more articles like them. Other letters were from amateur photographers who were having troubles of their own with the developers they were using and their methods of processing film. Then there were the usual letters from amateurs with an experimental bent who had theorized about the formulas given in CAMERA CRAFT and had changed things to suit themselves and then wondered why certain things happened. Photography is a science of chemistry besides being an art. We are not all chemists and we do not all have fine laboratories in which to conduct our work. Most of the fine grain developing is done in the kitchen sink. It is possible for the amateur kitchen photographer to have negatives as free from imperfections as those developed in the finest laboratory. On the other hand, it is possible for the worker in the finest laboratory to have a lot of troubles also. It may be well to enumerate some of the troubles which might confront us.

One of the prime reasons why we have such poor negatives when we develop them ourselves is because of impure water. Water is a chemical and is just as important a chemical as any of the other chemicals in the developer or fixing bath. Its purity should be beyond question. Water varies according to the territory through which it passes in its flow from the mountains to the sea. If it flows through lime rock, it will have an excess of alkali. It may have chlorine or sulphur or a host of other chemicals, and if it does, it is unfit for use in developing solutions. Chlorine, for example, will prevent developers containing paraphenylenediamine from acting. Sulphur and certain alkalis will soften the gelatin to such an extent that it will be ruined. The purity of water used in developing solutions is much more important than the purity of the water you drink. This is true of most of the other chemicals used in photography. The purity of water is no problem if distilled water is used for compounding all developing formulas.

The compounding of a formula is of the utmost importance. No chemical should be added to a solution until all the other chemicals in the solution have been dissolved. Certain chemicals will not dissolve in the presence of other chemicals. Metol, for instance. should be dissolved before sulphite is dissolved. Glycin, on the other hand, should not be added until the sulphite has been dissolved. Chemical formulas are usually listed in the order in which they are to be dissolved. It should be one of the first lessons taught the beginner in photography that all formulas should be dissolved in the order given. This will eliminate precipitates forming and certain chemicals from refusing entirely to act.

A developer should be stored in a place with a fairly even temperature. The temperature should not be allowed to drop to the freezing point in winter and then be raised for use, nor should it be allowed to reach 90° Fahrenheit in summer and then be cooled for use. The developer should be stored in a place with a fairly even temperature in winter, and in summer the bottle containing the developer should be wrapped with a layer or two of blotting paper and kept in a tray of water. The evaporation of the water from the blotter will maintain a temperature of from eight to ten degrees less than the prevailing temperature of the air. Hence, it is possible to store the bottle containing the developer in a comparatively cool place during the hottest days of summer and still maintain a temperature of approximately 70° Fahrenheit which is the best temperature for developers containing paraphenylenediamine and glycin.

The development process is a result of oxidation of the chemicals in the developing solution. This oxidation is accelerated by oxygen in the air and water. If the developing solution is allowed to stand open for any great length of time, it will be subjected to a continual stream of fresh oxygen, and its life will be materially shortened. A developing solution should, therefore, be stored in a closed bottle with very little air in the bottle. If it is desired to make a supply of developer, it should be stored in a number of small bottles instead of just one large bottle. For example, one gallon of developer is best stored in eight sixteen ounce bottles instead of a one-gallon bottle. Paraphenylenediamine-glycin developers do not have to be stored in brown or blue bottles; in fact, Dr. Sampson has proved that these developers showed some improvement in quality when stored in clear bottles and subjected to direct sunlight for several days. The writer has made several tests and has found this to be a fact.

A developing solution has a definite life. A developing solution will correctly develop just so many square inches of film and no more. The amount of film a developer will correctly develop depends entirely upon its composition. Too many fine grain developers are overworked. This is probably not a fault of the amateur photographer; the fault actually lies with the salesman behind the counter who is anxious to sell a bottle of his pet developer. The development process liberates silver and bromide from the film. The bromide is a restrainer and its action is to withhold detail in the shadows from the film; in other words, a developing solution containing a large quantity of bromide will develop less shadow detail than a developer containing little or no bromide. Prolonged developement will not do anything more than build up density in the highlights. For this reason developers claiming extraordinary life should be looked upon with a certain amount of doubt. With each Champlin formula shown in the back of this book, there is a figure showing how many ounces of developer are required for ten rolls of 35 mm miniature film. Any attempt to develop more film than the amount shown by these figures will result in a definite loss of emulsion speed. This loss in emulsion speed cannot be accurately gauged because there is no way for the amateur photographer to know exactly how much silver and bromide have been dissolved into the solution. This loss in emulsion speed is something which happens with any developer. No one has been able to compound a developer with an indefinite life.

Another source of great trouble is the fixing bath. Fine grain developed negatives should not be fixed in the common packaged acid fixing bath unless a hardening stop bath has been used. The chemicals in a para-phenylenediamine-glycin developer will quickly break down any fixing bath. As soon as there is any deterioration in the fixing bath, there will be an additional agglomeration of the silver grains in the emulsion. The fixing bath then can be a contributing factor to a coarse grain structure.

The fixing bath can also create the troublesome phenomenon known as reticulation. Reticulation is a result of the rapid expansion and contraction of the gelatin. If the development process is conducted at

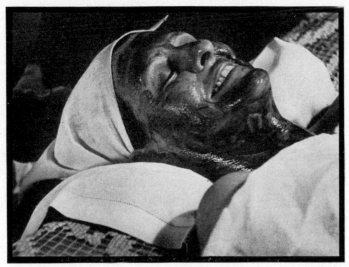

"*Mud Pack*" J. E. *Grant*

Contax; 85 mm. Triotar F:4; Super X exposed at Weston 32, by Mazda light; developed in Champlin #15.

"*Perfect development is the cornerstone of photographic achievement and such an advance as the Champlin formulas must not be overlooked.*"

—*J. E. Grant*

70° Fahrenheit and the fixing or washing at higher or lower temperatures, there will be an instantaneous contraction of the gelatin into little wrinkles and these wrinkles will remain after the film has dried and will ruin the negative for printing purposes. The fixing bath should contain a hardener so that the film emulsion will be completely hardened and less liable to injury through changes of temperature. The chemicals carried from the developer to the fixing bath will quickly break down the fixing bath. This breakdown usually occurs long before it is apparent to the average kitchen photographer. One of the most important safeguards against reticulation in fixing films is a fresh fixing bath.

The use of a hardening stop bath between developing and fixation is a good practice. The hardening stop bath will neutralize some of the chemicals carried from the developer to the fixing bath and in addition, will harden the film and make it immune to the effects of the fixing bath and final wash. A good hardening stop bath can be compounded with:

Water	16 ounces	500 ccs
Sodium Bisulphite	¼ ounce	7 grams
Potassium Chrome Alum	¼ ounce	7 grams

The films should be rinsed for about one minute in this solution and then transferred to the fixing bath. This hardening stop bath can be made up by the amateur photographer who is not equipped with scales for weighing by simply using one-half teaspoonful each of sodium bisulphite and potassium chrome alum in a pint of water. Extreme accuracy is not necessary in measuring out this bath. This bath will not keep longer than one day. It should be used and then discarded. The hardening-fixing bath can be compounded from any good formula containing, besides the hypo, sodium sulphite, acetic acid, and potassium alum. An excellent hardening-fixing bath can be made with plain hypo crystals and Velox Liquid Hardener in the proportions recommended by the Eastman Kodak Company on each bottle of hardener. Fixation should take twenty minutes because that much time is required for the potassium alum to fully harden the gelatin emulsion of the film. When films are first immersed in the fixing bath, they should be agitated in order that no air-bells or bubbles can form and remain on the surface of the emulsion. Fine grain developing formulas usually contain chemicals that react and form a gas when first immersed in the fixing bath. This gas will remain upon the surface of the film in the form of bubbles or air-bells unless the films are agitated. These air-bells or bubbles will leave little round marks upon the film and will be a source of annoyance in printing and will require retouching of the print.

In drying films, care should be exercised that no dust is allowed to settle upon the surface of the emulsion. Dust is usually a result of carelessness and is a source of annoyance at all times. If dust is in the camera or is allowed to settle upon film before it is loaded into the camera, it will prevent the image formed by the lens from affecting the light-sensitive silver directly behind it, and there will be little clear irregular spots upon the film. These will form little black marks upon the final print. In loading 35 mm film into cartridges, work as quickly as possible so that dust will not have much time to settle upon the film. A film winder of some sort will prevent many dust blemishes upon film.

While upon the subject of film, it may be well to caution users of 35 mm motion picture film against the practice of buying short ends of film. Many camera shops sell this film. It is really second-hand film and in common with second-hand goods, it sometimes has defects. It seems silly to buy a camera costing one or two hundred dollars and then attempt to save a cent or two on the film required for eight pictures. The use of film in film manufacturers' unopened packages, be it single cartridges or one or two hundred foot lots, is strongly urged. Remember this, that you cannot buy one hundred feet of film at one-half the price which motion picture studios pay when they buy one hundred hundred thousand feet of film.

Several of the chemicals required for the formulas given in this book are not commonly used in photography. Consequently photographic dealers are not likely to have them in stock, at least until they have had time to acquire them after the publication of this volume.

The writer has no interest in directing purchases to any particular source, but advises that care be taken to secure high grade chemicals.

The Edwal Laboratories, Inc., 732 Federal St., Chicago, Ill., supply a good grade paraphenylenediamine (pure base) and glycin.

Such a large and reliable chemical supply firm as Mallinckrodt has branches in the principal cities and will be able to supply everything required on request. If the address of such a branch is not available the Chemical Supply Co., 6324 Santa Monica Blvd., Los Angeles, Calif., can supply the individual chemicals or the Champlin #15 developer ready-mixed.

The author will be much interested in learning of the results obtained by those who follow the recommendations given in this book. He is always willing to help the serious student of fine grain problems, but asks that readers refrain from sending to him questions on other subjects which can readily be answered by others. Communications should be addressed to Harry Champlin, 9708 Santa Monica Blvd., Beverly Hills, Calif.

APPENDIXES

APPENDIX A

Amateur Films

Correctly exposed negatives will develop to a perfect contrast in a definite time. This time factor is dependent upon the temperature of the developing solution, the composition of the developing solution, and the developing characteristics of the film emulsion. Some films require as much as four times as long as others to develop to a standard contrast.

Certain allowances must be made for films which have a scratch-proof coating. This surface hardening or scratch-proofing is something like pre-hardening, and it prevents the solution from penetrating the emulsion so readily. This naturally results in an increase in time required to develop these films to normal contrast.

Filmpacks require twenty - five per cent more time to attain correct contrast because the surface of these films are coated to prevent scratching when drawn around to the back of the pack.

Certain miniature films packed in daylight cartridges are also surface hardened so that they will not be scratched by the felt light-proofing of the cartridge. These films usually require about twenty per cent more time to attain normal contrast.

In the following list films are classified according to their developing times. The number in the first column opposite each film indicates a classification and corresponds to the numbers opposite the developing times given with most of the developing formulas in the next section of this book. Films marked with one asterisk (*) require twenty per cent more time and those marked with two asterisks (**) require twenty-five per cent more time than the times given with the various formulas in the chapter following.

The emulsion speeds in combination with two developing formulas are also given. The figures in columns two and three represent the Weston speeds of the various films when used with the Eastman formula D-76 and the Champlin formula #15. These emulsion speeds are correct for Weston settings at mid-day. There is, of course, a variation in the light from hour to hour. This variation is not only in the intensity of light but is also in the color balance of the light. For this reason there should be a change in the setting of a Weston meter in accordance with the time of day. For example, Du Pont Superior film which has an emulsion speed at noon of 24 with Eastman formula D-76 and of 64 with Champlin #15, will have only one-half these speeds at 5 o'clock in the afternoon. The meter should be set to 16 and 32 respectively at 5 o'clock in the afternoon. Meters are generally more sensitive to light with a predominance of red, orange, and yellow, and this accounts for the failure of many amateur photographers in minimum exposure photography. From this it will be seen that the use of a meter should be tempered with a certain amount of judgment and experience.

The figures in column four give the Weston emulsion speeds under mazda light with the Champlin #15 developer.

Comparison Table of Speed Values

Scheiner°	Din°	H & D	Weston
14	7/10	159	3
15	8/10	200	4
16	9/10	252	5
17	10/10	318	6
18	11/10	400	8
19	12/10	504	10
20	13/10	635	12
21	14/10	800	16
22	15/10	1000	20
23	16/10	1270	24
24	17/10	1600	32
25	18/10	2020	40
26	19/10	2540	50
27	20/10	3200	64

Film Speeds

	Speed of Development	D-76	Weston Daylight Emulsion Speed with #15	Weston Mazda Emulsion Speed with #15
Agfa Films				
**Plenachrome Roll Film	2	16	24	12
**Plenachrome Filmpack	2	16	24	12
Supersensitive Plenachrome Cut Film	2	20	32	16
Superpan. Roll Film	2	24	40	20
Superpan. Filmpack	2	24	40	20
Finopan Fine-Grain	2	16	20	12
Barnet Sensichrome Roll Film	2	24	40	
Defender Films				
Pan. X-fast	2	24	40	20
Pan	1	12	16	
Pentagon	3	16	24	
XF Pan. Special	3	24	40	20
Eastman Kodak Films				
Super Sensitive Panchromatic Roll Film	3	24	40	20
**Super Sensitive Panchromatic Filmpack	3	24	40	20
Verichrome Roll Film	3	16	24	
**Verichrome Filmpack	3	16	24	
Panatomic Roll Film	2	16	20	12
**Panatomic Filmpack	2	16	20	12
Super Sensitive Panchromatic Cut Film	3	24	50	20
Ortho Press Cut Film	2	16	32	
Commercial Panchromatic Cut Film	1	12	16	
Portrait Panchromatic Cut Film	2	16	32	
**Gevaert Superchrom Filmpack	2	32	40	
Mimosa Fine Grain Film	3	8	16	
Mimosa Extreme Film	3	16	24	
Perutz Fine Grain	3	16	24	
Perutz Peromnia	3	24	40	20
Perutz Persenso	3	24	40	
Selo Fine Grain Panchro. Film	2	24	32	
Selo Hypersen. Pan. Film	2	32	64	24
Selo Infra Red Roll Film	2	2	6	
Selochrome Roll Film	2	32	40	
Selochrome Filmpack	2	32	40	

	Speed of Development	D-76	Daylight Emulsion Speed with #15	Mazda Emulsion Speed with #15
Zeiss Roll Film	3	8	16	
**Zeiss Filmpack	3	8	16	
Zeiss Pernox	2	24	32	
Zeiss Pernox Pan	2	24	32	20

35 mm Miniature Films

	Speed of Development	D-76	Daylight Emulsion Speed with #15	Mazda Emulsion Speed with #15
Agfa Ansco 35 mm Finopan	4	12	16	
Agfa Ansco 35 mm Plenachrome Fine Gr.	3	16	20	12
Agfa Ansco 35 mm Superpan	2	24	40	20
Agfa Ansco 35 mm Infra Red	3	5	8	
Cappelli Super Panchro	3	24	32	20
Du Pont 35 mm Superior Neg.	3	24	64	32
Du Pont 35 mm Infra D	2	8	12	
Du Pont 35 mm Micro Pan	1	4	6	
Gevaert 35 mm Fine-Grain	3	12	16	
Gevaert 35 mm Express	3	20	32	
Gevaert 35 mm Panchromosa	2	24	40	20
*Kodak 35 mm Super-X Pan	3	32	64	24
Kodak 35 mm Super Sensitive Pan.	3	24	40	20
*Kodak 35 mm Panatomic	2	16	20	16
Kodak 35 mm Background Pan.	4	12	16	
Mimosa Fine Grain	3	12	16	
Mimosa Extrema	3	24	40	20
*Perutz 35 mm Neo-Perseno	3	20	32	
*Perutz 35 mm Rectepan	2	10	16	
*Perutz 35 mm Peromnia	3	24	40	20
*Perutz 35 mm Perpantic	2	20	32	
Selo 35 mm Extra Fine-Grain Pan.	2	12	16	
Selo 35 mm Fine-Grain Hyper Pan.	2	24	40	
*Zeiss 35 mm Pernox	2	24	40	
*Zeiss 35 mm Pernox Pan	2	24	40	20

103

WARNING!

It may be well to say something about the purity of the chemicals used in the Champlin Formulas given in this book. Sodium sulphite should be as free as possible from alkalis. Paraphenylenediamine should be a pure base and not the hydrochloride. Glycin should be of the highest purity. Glycin is an unstable chemical and some manufacturers add to it a preservative in order that it will not deteriorate too rapidly. It should be very fluffy and have a faintly sweet odor. If it appears lumpy or has any trace of an acid odor, it should not be used. This is highly important because glycin plays a major part in all these formulas. Acid digallic (tannic) should be of the highest purity because ordinary grades sometimes contain iron or other impurities which have a detrimental effect upon the properties of the developer. For this reason this chemical, and the other acids recommended, should be of reagent quality and a photographer is urged to insist upon this quality when purchasing chemicals for these developers.

APPENDIX B

APPENDIX B

Developing Formulas

Perfect negatives are a result of correct exposure and correct development. No negative will be perfect if one of these two factors is faulty. Correct exposure must be based upon the emulsion speed of the film and the emulsion speed of the developer. The emulsion speed of the film-developer combination is the basis upon which the exposure must be made. Some developing formulas will develop all of the light-affected silver halide, while other developing formulas will not. For this reason some developers require more exposure than others in order that negatives will have normal density. The selection of a developer should be based upon certain required characteristics. The following list of developers is given in order that the composition and characteristics of a number of developers can be readily compared.

Each formula gives the composition of the developer. In compounding the solution the chemicals should be dissolved in the order given. Each chemical should be completely dissolved before the next one is added. The keeping qualities of the developers are given. This is highly important knowledge to any one attempting to use a developing solution more than once or over a period of time. The emulsion speed of the developer is given and this, too, is very important. Normally exposed negatives will develop to a perfect density in a developing solution with an emulsion speed of 100. If the emulsion speed of the developer is 50, negatives will have to be exposed twice as long in order to attain the same density. Thus, it is possible with the emulsion speed figures given with each developer to expose a negative correctly for that developer. The developing times given are for normal density negatives.

There is also given with each of the Champlin formulas a figure showing just how many ounces of developer are required to develop ten rolls of film correctly. This figure varies with the different developers and is a correct indication of the reduction ability of the different developers.

Agitation

All of the developing times which follow are based upon agitation at every 10% of the developing time. In other words if the developing time is 20 minutes agitation should take place every 2 minutes.

To determine the developing time for any given film in any given formula, turn to the table in Appendix A and look up the figure given in the first column opposite the film being used. Then turn to the formula in this section and use the developing time which appears opposite the same figure that accompanied the film in Appendix A. For example DuPont Superior is classified as 3 in Appendix A. If we turn to the Champlin #15 formula in Appendix B we see that films in classification 3 should be developed for 20 mins. at 70° F. or 18 mins. at 73° F.

Eastman D-76

Elon (metol)	29 grains	2 grams
Sodium Sulphite	3½ ounces	100 grams
Hydroquinone	72 grains	5 grams
Sodium Borate (borax)	29 grains	2 grams
Water	32 ounces	1000 ccs

This is a standard developer for large negatives. The grain structure is too coarse for 35 mm films. Keeping qualities: Good.
Emulsion speed: 100

Eastman D-76-d

Elon (metol)	29 grains	2 grams
Sodium Sulphite	3½ ounces	100 grams
Hydroquinone	72 grains	5 grams
Sodium Borate (borax)	120 grains	8 grams
Acid Boric crystals	120 grains	8 grams
Water	32 ounces	1000 ccs

This developer is also a standard for large negatives. The grain structure is too coarse for miniature films. Keeping qualities: Good.

Emulsion speed: 100

Paraphenylenediamine-Sulphite Formula

Water	20 ounces	1000 ccs
Paraphenylenediamine	90 grains	9 grams
Sodium Sulphite	525 grains	52 grams

This is probably the finest grained formula so far produced.

Keeping qualities: Very poor.

Emulsion speed: 14.

The tremendous exposure increase necessary with this developer makes its use impractical.

Metol-Paraphenylenediamine Formula
A. Seyewitz Low Contrast Formula

Water	20 ounces	1000 ccs
Sodium Sulphite	1¼ ounces	60 grams
Metol	45 grains	5 grams
Paraphenylenediamine	90 grains	10 grams
Tribasic Sodium Phosphate	30 grains	3.5 grams
Potassium Bromide	10 grains	1 gram

This developer was brought out because it gave an increased emulsion speed over the Sease #3 formula.

Grain structure: fine and even.

Keeping qualities: poor.

Emulsion speed: 50

Developing times: 65°

1— 7½ min.
2—11¼ min.
3—15   min.
4—6½ min.

Metol-Paraphenylenediamine Developer
A. Seyewitz Low Contrast Formula

Water	20	ounces	1000	ccs
Sodium Sulphite	1¼	ounces	60	grams
Metol	90	grains	10	grams
Paraphenylenediamine	45	grains	5	grams
Hydroquinone	15	grains	1.5	grams
Tribasic Sodium Phosphate	45	grains	5	grams
Potassium Bromide	10	grains	1	grams

This developer was brought out because it gave an increased emulsion speed over the Sease #3 formula.

Grain structure: fine and even.
Keeping qualities: poor.

Emulsion speed: 50

Developing times: 65°

```
1 — 9½ min.
2—14¼ min.
3—19   min.
4— 7½ min.
```

Sease #3 Formula

Water	32 ounces	1000 ccs
Sodium Sulphite	3 ounces	90 grams
Paraphenylenediamine	154 grains	10 grams
Glycin	88 grains	6 grams

This is a standard fine grain developer for miniature negatives.

The grain structure is very fine and very even.
Keeping qualities: fair.

Emulsion speed: 28.

Developing times: 68°

```
1          7
2         12
3         24
```

Lowering the quantity of glycin will create an even finer grain structure and will give a corresponding decrease in emulsion speed.

Edwal-12

Water (distilled)	32 ounces	1 litre
Metol	90 grains	6 grams
Sodium Sulphite (anhydrous)	3 ounces	90 grams
Paraphenylenediamine (pure base)	150 grains	10 grams
Glycin	75 grains	5 grams

This is one of the most popular and widely used of fine grain formulas, and is probably the best of the developers containing paraphenylenediamine-glycin-metol.

Keeping qualities: good

Emulsion speed: 140*

Developing times:		65°	70°	75°
	1	12	10	7½
	2	18	15	11
	3	22	18	14
	4	10	8	6

*This rating applies to Panatomic, Du Pont Superior, and Finopan. The rating should be somewhat lower for most other films. Make test outlined in Chapter 3.

Edwal-20

Water (distilled)	32 ounces	1 litre
Gradol	75 grains	5 grams
Paraphenylenediamine (pure base)	150 grains	10 grams
Sodium Sulphite (anhydrous)	3 ounces	90 grams
Glycin	75 grains	5 grams

Gradol (gray-dol) a product of the Edwal Laboratories, recently placed on the market.

This formula was worked out to give finer grain than is possible with Edwal-12, without the sacrifice of good graduation.

Keeping qualities: good

Emulsion speed: 70

Developing times:		65°	70°	75°
	1	14	12	19
	2	22	13	14
	3	26	22	18
		11	9	7

Champlin #5

Sodium Sulphite	¾	ounce	22.5	grams
Acid Salicyclic	4	grains	.3	grams
Sodium Bisulphite	8	grains	.5	grams
Paraphenylenediamine	59	grains	4	grams
Glycin	59	grains	4	grams
Water	8	ounces	250	ccs

For use take one part of the above stock solution and fifteen parts of water.

Keeping qualities: Perfect.

Emulsion speed: 55

Developing times:		65°	70°	73°
	1		32	`
	2	Not	35	Not
	3	Recom-	50	Recom-
	4	mended	28	mended.

Amount required to develop 10 rolls of 35 mm film: 10 ounces.

Champlin #6 Formula

Sodium Sulphite	¾	ounce	22.5	grams
Acid Salicylic	4	grains	.3	grams
Sodium Bisulphite	8	grains	.5	grams
Paraphenylenediamine	59	grains	4	grams
Glycin	59	grains	4	grams
Metol	15	grains	1	gram
Water	8	ounces	250	ccs

For use take one part of the above and fifteen parts of water.

Keeping qualities: Perfect.

Emulsion speed: 70

Developing times:		65°	70°	73°
	1		32	°
	2	Not	35	Not
	3	Recom-	50	Recom-
	4	mended	28	mended.

Amount required to develop 10 rolls of 35 mm film: 10 ounces:

Champlin #7 Formula

Water	.20	ounces	1000	ccs
Metol	.25	grains	2.5	grams
Sodium Sulphite	1	ounce	45	grams
Acid Benzoic	9	grains	1	gram
Acid Salicylic	4	grains	0.5	gram
Acid Boric	.25	grains	2.5	grams
Glycin	1/4	ounce	11.5	grams
Paraphenylenediamine	1/4	ounce	11.5	grams

Keeping qualities: Excellent.

Emulsion speed: 140

Developing times:		65°	70°	73°
1			13	12
2		Not	16	15
3		Recom-	19½	18
4		mended	9½	8

Amount required to develop 10 rolls of 35 mm film: 24 ounces.

Champlin #8 Formula

Water	.64	ounces	2000	ccs
Sodium Sulphite	3½	ounces	100	grams
Acid Pyrogallic	3/4	ounces	34.5	grams
Acid Benzoic	.36	grains	2.4	grams
Acid Salicylic	.15	grains	1	gram
Acid Boric	.75	grains	7.5	grams
Glycin	3/4	ounce	34.5	grams
Paraphenylenediamine	3/4	ounce	34.5	grams

Keeping qualities: Perfect.

Emulsion speed: 130

Developing times:		65°	70°	73°
1			14	
2		Not	17	Not
3		Recom-	20	Recom-
4		mended.	10	mended.

Amount required to develop 10 rolls 35 mm film: 16 ounces.

Champlin #9 Formula

Water	20	ounces	1000	ccs
Rubinol (Defender)	32	grains	3.5	grams
Sodium Sulphite	1½	ounces	60	grams
Acid Benzoic	18	grains	2	grams
Acid Salicylic	4	grains	0.5	gram
Acid Boric	25	grains	2.5	grams
Acid Digallic (Tannic)	9	grains	1	gram
Glycin	¼	ounce	11.5	grams
Paraphenylenediamine	¼	ounce	11.5	grams
Alcohol Iso Propyl 97%	1	ounce	50	ccs

Keeping qualities: Perfect.

Emulsion speed: 160

Developing times:		65°	70°	73°
	1		13	
	2	Not	16	Not
	3	Recom-	19½	Recom-
	4	mended.	10	mended.

Amount required to develop 10 rolls of 35 mm film: 31 ounces.

Champlin #10 Formula

Water	64	ounces	2000	ccs
Sodium Sulphite	3½	ounces	100	grams
Acid Pyrogallic	¾	ounce	34.5	grams
Acid Benzoic	36	grains	2.4	grams
Acid Salicylic	15	grains	1	gram
Acid Boric	75	grains	7.5	gram
Glycin	¾	ounce	34.5	grams
Paraphenylenediamine	¾	ounce	34.5	grams
Alcohol Iso Propyl 97%	3	ounces	90	ccs
Sodium Sulphate	3½	ounces	100	grams

Keeping qualities: Perfect.

Emulsion speed: 130

Developing times:		65°	70°	73°
	1		14	
	2	Not	17	Not
	3	Recom-	20	Recom-
	4	mended.	10	mended.

Amount required to develop 10 rolls 35 mm film: 16 ounces.

Champlin #11 Formula

Water	20	ounces	1000	ccs
Rubinol (Defender)	32	grains	3.5	grams
Sodium Sulphite	1½	ounces	60	grams
Acid Benzoic	18	grains	2	grams
Acid Salicylic	4	grains	0.5	gram
Acid Boric	25	grains	2.5	grams
Acid Digallic	9	grains	1	gram
Glycin	¼	ounce	11.5	grams
Paraphenylenediamine	¼	ounce	11.5	grams
Alcohol Iso Propyl 97%	1	ounce	50	ccs
Nickel Chloride	20	grains	2	grams

Keeping qualities: Good.

Emulsion speed: 180

Developing times:	65°	70°	73°
1		13	11
2	Not	16	14
3	Recom-	20	18
4	mended	11	9½

Amount required to develop 10 rolls of 35 mm. film: 40 ounces.

Champlin #15 Formula

Water	20	ounces	1000	ccs
Rubinol or Pyro	32	grains	3.5	grams
Sodium Sulphite	1½	ounces	60	grams
Acid Benzoic	12	grains	1.2	grams
Acid Salicylic	4	grains	0.5	grams
Acid Boric	25	grains	2.5	grams
Acid Digallic (Tannic)	9	grains	1	gram
Glycin	¼	ounce	11.5	grams
Paraphenylenediamine	¼	ounce	11.5	grams
Alcohol Iso Propyl 97%	1	ounce	50	ccs
Nickel & Ammonium Sulphate	10	grains	1	gram

Keeping qualities: Perfect.

Emulsion speed: 200

Developing times:	65°	70°	73°
1		13	11
2	Not	16	14
3	Recom-	20	18
4	mended	11	9½

Amount required to develop 10 rolls of 35 mm film: 32 ounces.

This is probably the best developing formula offered for miniature camera work. The keeping qualitiees are excellent. The grain structure is very fine. The emulsion speed is very high and this developer lacks those certain idiosyncrasies common to most fine grain developing formulas. The amateur photographer is strongly urged to try this developer because if he does try it, he will adopt it as the standard for all his work.

In compounding formula No. 15, dissolve the chemicals in the order shown. Dissolve the pyro first, then the sulphite and the acids and glycin in about two-thirds of the water. The paraphenylenediamine should be dissolved separately in a small quantity of water which has been heated to 180 degrees fahrenheit and should then be added to the developer. After the developer has cooled to 70 degrees fahrenheit, dissolve the nickel and ammonium sulphate in a small quantity of water—one ounce, and add slowly to the developer. A precipitate will form which should be stirred into the developer. This precipitate will be milky, but will clarify immediately upon stirring. The developer should then be filtered through the filter paper commonly used by chemists; a coarse cloth or absorbent cotton will not suffice for this purpose. The alcohol can be added to the solution at any time after it has been cooled to 70 degrees fahrenheit. The resulting quantity of developer can vary as much as ten per cent in volume over the amount of water shown without any noticeable difference in final result.

Develop for the times given and increase time 2 minutes for each additional roll of film developed.

It will be noted that the #15 formula reads "Rubinol or Pyro". Rubinol is definitely required for the #9 developer but it has been found that in the presence of nickel and ammonium sulphate there is no discernible difference in the action of these two chemicals, consequently they may be used interchangably in the #15 formula.

CHEMICALS

General Chemicals, Raw Materials,
and Developing Substances Used in
Fine Grain Developing Formulae.

By

SAMUEL FOX, Pharm. D.

FOREWORD

Every aspect of photography requires a scientific approach, especially as we begin now to understand more fully the intricate processes that take place in producing a photographic negative and the prints therefrom. Fine artistry has often been impaired or even nullified as a result of underrating the importance of the chemical processes involved and the chemicals used in photography. In the following pages we shall attempt to deal with one of the problems of photography from a purely chemical point of view. Although knowledge of chemistry is desirable, we shall attempt to deal with the subject in such a manner so that any photographer can read this with benefit.

One of the most important functions of the discriminating photographer is his choice of the materials with which he brings out the desired effect of his exposures which represent his personal artistry. As the technique of the photographer has become more complex, a critical demand for finer grade chemicals has arisen. In the following pages we shall enumerate some of the chemicals commonly used by the photographer including their various chemical properties, their applications and functions, and the highest purity necessary for best results.

SAMUEL FOX, Pharm. D,

General Recommendations

We recommend that special care be used in weighing the chemicals. We found that good white vegetable parchment to be placed on the scale pans is safe, as it is neutral in reaction. Stainless steel spatulas or hard rubber ones are also indicated, and glass stirring rods and glass vessels for mixing.

Dissolve the various chemicals in the solutions with the least amount of heat necessary. Distilled water is recommended throughout.

A Harvard Trip Balance is recommended. It is of good size and capacity and very reasonable for that type of balance. Prices range from nine to twelve dollars for single and double beam. The beams are usually marked with the metric system. On this balance you can weigh with an accuracy of one decigram.

METRIC EQUIVALENTS

Volume

1 minim (water)	—	0.06161 cc.
1 fl. dr.	—	3.70 cc.
1 fl. oz.	—	29.5737 cc.
1 Apoth. oz. (water)	—	31.1035 cc.
1 pint	—	0.4732 liter
1 qt.	—	0.9464 liter
1 gal. (U.S.)	—	3.7854 liters
1 cc.	—	16.23 minims (water)
1 cc.	—	0.2702 fl. dr.
1 cc.	—	0.0338 fl. oz.
1 liter	—	1.0567 qt.
1 liter	—	0.2642 gal.
1 liter	—	33.84 fl. oz.

Weight

1 grain	—	64.7989 Mgm.
1 oz. Avoir.	—	28.3495 Gm.
1 oz. Troy	—	31.1035 Gm.
1 lb. Avoir.	—	0.4536 kilo.
1 lb. Troy	—	0.3732 kilo.
1 lb. Avoir.	—	453.5924 Gm.
1 Mgm.	—	0.01543 grn.
1 Gm.	—	15.432 grn.
1 Kilo.	—	33.814 fl. oz.
1 Kilo.	—	2.205 lb. Avoir.
1 Kilo.	—	2.679 lb. Troy
1 Kilo.	—	35.274 oz. Avoir.
1 Kilo.	—	32.151 oz. Troy
Gm. ÷ 28.35	—	oz. Avoir.

ABBREVIATIONS

Avoirdupois

fl. dr.	—fluid dram
fl. oz.	—fluid ounce
qt.	—quart
lb.	—pound
grn.	—grain
Apoth.	—Apothecaries measure
Avoir.	—Avoirdupois measure

Metric

cc.	—cubic centimeter
Mgm.	—Miligram (.001)
Gm.	—Gram
Kilo.	—Kilogram (1000)

ORGANIC REDUCING AGENTS

A Comparison of the Organic Reducing Substances in General Use Today

Name	Formula	Characteristics				Molecular Weight
		Reduction Potential	Effect of Temp. Change	Solubility	Deterioration	
		(Numbers represent degree)				
Amidol (Diaminophenol hydrochlorid?)	$HOC_6H_3(NH_2)_2 2HCl$	30	5	3	10	197.05
Glycin (Para-oxy-phenylglycine)	$C_6H_4(OH)NH\,CH_2COOH$	2	4	0	1	151.08
Hydroquinone or Hydrochinon (Quinol or paradioxybenzene)	$C_6H_4(OH)_2$	1	6	4	2	110.03
Metol or Elon (Mono-methyl-paramidophenol-sulphate)	$C_6H_4OH.NHCH_3, \frac{1}{2}H_2SO_4$	6	3	5	3	172.16
Ortol (Sulphate of monomethyl-ortho-amidophenol with hydroquinone)	$C_3H_4(OH)_2 \div C_6H_4OHNHCH_3 \div (H_2SO_4/2)$	2	4	3	2	282.17
Paramidolphenol (Rodinal) (Amino-phenol-p)	$C_6H_4OHNH_2$	3	2	5	1	109.06
Paraphenylenediamine (Diamino-benzene-p)	$C_6H_4(NH_2)_2$	0	5			108.11
Pyrocatechin (Ortho-dihydrox-benzene-O.) (Catechol)	$C_6H_4(OH)_2$-ortho	2	2	5		110.05
Pyro or Pyrogallol (Pyrogallic acid) (Tri-oxy-benzene)	$C_6H_3(OH)_3$	5	10	10	10	126.05

AUXILIARY CHEMICALS

A Reference List of General Chemicals Used in Photography.

Name	Formula	Solubility in H_2O	Molecular Weight
Preservers			
Sodium sulphite	Na_2SO_3	Easily	126.05
Keepers			
Potassium metabisulphite (Potassium sulfite-pyro)	$K_2S_2O_5$	Readily	222.32
Sodium bisulphite (Sodium sulphite-acid)	$NaHSO_3$	Slowly	104.00
Accelerators			
Ammonia Water	NH_4OH	Miscible	34.03
Borax (Sodium tetraborate)	$Na_2B_4O_7$ 10 H_2O	Readily	381.43
Glycerin	$C_3H_8O_3$	Miscible	92.06
Sodium carbonate	$Na_2CO_3.H_2O$	Readily	124.02
Sodium hydroxide	$NaOH$	Readily	40.00
Potassium carbonate	K_2CO_3	Readily	138.20
Potassium hydroxide	KOH	Readily	56.11
Restrainers			
Potassium bromide	KBr	Readily	119.02
Potassium iodide	KI	Very readily	166.03
Sodium chloride (Common salt)	$NaCl$	Easily	58.45
Other Agents			
Acetic acid	CH_3COOH	Readily	60.03
Alcohol (Ethyl) or (grain)	C_2H_5OH	Miscible	46.00
Boric acid (Boracic acid)	H_2BO_3	Readily	61.84
Citric acid	$H_3C_6H_5O_7.H_2O$	Readily	210.08
Formaldehyde	CH_2O	Easily	30.02
Potassium alum	$AlK(SO_4)_2.12H_2O$	Slowly	474.41
Potassium chrome alum	$K_2Cr_2(SO_4)_4 24H_2O$	Slowly	998.95
Sodium sulphate	$Na_2SO_4 \div 10H_2O$	Readily	322.05
Sodium thiosulphate (Hypo)	$Na_2S_2O_3$ 5H_2O	Easily	248.19
Water (Distilled)	H_2O	....	18.02

ACETONE
(CH₃)₂CO

$(CH_3)_2CO$

Physical Characteristics : Clear, colorless, highly inflammable liquid, characteristically ethereal odor.

Molecular Weight : 58.05
Specific Gravity : about 0.798°
Boiling Point : 56.48° Centigrade
Solubility : In water, ether, and alcohol.

Maximum Limits of Impurities

Non-Volatile	0.001%
Precipitated by H_2O	0.000%
Acids (as $HC_2H_3O_2$)	0.003%
Alkaline Substances (as NH_3)	0.001%
Aldehyde	0.000%
Subs. Reducing $KMnO_4$	0.000%

Conforms to A. C. S. * specifications.

Acetone can be used as a substitute for alkalis in certain developers. The addition of 3% acetone to acid developing solutions will act as a tremendous energizer of the solutions.

*—A. C. S. stands for American Chemical Society.

ACID ACETIC, 99.5%
CH₃COOH

CH_3COOH

Physical Characteristics: Clear colorless liquid; strong pungent odor; vapor is inflammable.

Molecular Weight : 60.03
Freezing Point : 15.8° Centigrade
Boiling Point : 118.1° Centigrade
Solubility : In water, alcohol, ether, chloroform and glycerine.

Maximum Limits of Impurities

Non-Volatile	0.0005%
Chloride (Cl)	0.0001%
Sulphate (SO_4)	0.0002%
Iron (Fe)	0.0002%
Other Heavy Metals (as Pb)	0.0000%
Subs. Reducing $KMnO_4$	0.000 %
Subs. Precipitated by H_2O	0.000 %

Acetic acid is used in the preparation of acid fixing baths. It is used to counteract or neutralize the alkalis carried in the film emulsion from the developer to the fixing bath. The strength commonly used in photography is 28% with a specific gravity of 1.038. This strength can be prepared from glacial acetic acid by diluting three parts of glacial acetic acid with eight parts of water. Lower grades of acetic acid often contain oxidizable impurities and considerable quantities of iron. Acetic acid should be kept in dark, tightly stoppered bottles.

ACID BENZOIC
$C_6H_5CO_2H$

Physical Characteristics :	Colorless lustrous needles or scales.
Molecular Weight	: 122.05
Specific Gravity	: 1.2659
Melting Point	: 121.25° Centigrade
Boiling Point	: 249.2° Centigrade
Solubility	: In alcohol and ether; slightly soluble in water; readily soluble in 10% sodium sulphite solution.

Maximum Limits of Impurities

Chlorine Compounds (Cl)	0.001%
Ignition Residue	0.002 %
Heavy Metals (as Pb)	0.0002%

Conforms to A.C.S. specifications.

Acid benzoic can be used as a restrainer in fine grain formulae and it also exerts a slight hardening action upon gelatin. The amount of acid benzoic should not exceed 1½ grams per litre of developer. More than this amount will prolong developing time beyond reasonable limits. Acid benzoic is a stable organic acid and keeps well with ordinary care.

ACID BORIC
H₃BO₃

Physical Characteristics : Colorless transparent crystals
or white powder.

Molecular Weight   : 61.84
Specific Gravity   : 1.4347
Melting Point   : 184° Centigrade
Solubility   : In water, alcohol, glycerine,
and volatile oils.

Maximum Limits of Impurities

Insoluble in Alcohol	0.00 %
Non-Volatile with Methanol	0.05 %
Chloride (Cl)	0.001 %
Phosphate (PO₄)	0.001 %
Sulphate (SO₄)	0.010 %
Arsenic (As)	0.0003%
Calcium (Ca)	0.003 %
Iron (Fe)	0.001 %
Other Heavy Metals (as Pb)	0.0005%

Conforms to A.C.S. specifications.

Acid boric is used in developers containing pyro and
its derivatives, and as a restrainer, and in developing
formulae as a buffer in order that the acid-alkalinity of
the solution may be maintained. If the concentration
of acid boric is too high, it will act as an effective stop
bath and the developing solution will be useless. Acid
boric is a very stable inorganic compound, keeps well,
is very slightly affected by heat or light. and ordinary
care is sufficient in storing.

ACID CITRIC
H₃C₆H₅O₇.H₂O

Physical Characteristics : Colorless, odorless crystals.
Molecular Weight   : 210.08
Specific Gravity   : 1.542
Melting Point   : 153° Centrigrade
Solubility   : In water, alcohol, and ether.

Maximum Limits of Impurities

Residue on Ignition	0.020 %
Insoluble Matter	0.00 %
Oxalate (C₂O₄)	0.05 %
Phosphate (PO₄)	0.001 %
Sulphate (SO₄)	0.002 %
Tartrate (C₄H₆O₆)	0.2 %

Calcium (Ca) .... 0.005 %
Iron (Fe) 0.0005%
Other Heavy Metals (as Pb) 0.0005%
Conforms to A.C.S. specifications.

Acid citric can be used as a preservative in some developing solutions and as a restrainer in others. It can be used in pyro developers and will prevent the formation of the yellow pyro stain. Acid citric can be used in hardening-fixing solutions. One part of acid citric is equivalent to two parts of acid acetic 28%. Acid citric can be substituted for acid acetic glacial weight for weight. Citric acid is a stable organic acid, keeps well if not exposed to heat, and effloresces in warm air.

ACID DIGALLIC (Tannin)

$$C_{14}H_{10}O_9$$

Physical Characteristics :	Yellowish white to light brown amorphous b u l k y powder.
Molecular Weight	: 322
Melting Point	: Decomposes at 210° Centigrade.
Solubility	: In water and alcohol; slightly soluble in ether; soluble in glycerin with the aid of heat.

Maximum Limit of Impurities

Ignition Residue .... 0.10 %
Sugar and Dextrin 0.000%
Water .... 12.0 %

Acid digallic has been recommended as a hardening agent in the developing solution. The action of this chemical in a developer is to harden the developed image in proportion to the amount of reduced silver in the image. This hardened image forms a base upon which dyes can be mordanted. This organic acid gives blue or green colors or precipitates with iron (ferric) salts, and precipitates solutions of gelatin and albumin. Indications are that this acid has many photographic possibilities. It should be kept in a dry cool place, well corked, and away from metallic contacts.

ACID HYDROCHLORIC, 36-37%
HCl

Physical Characteristics :	Clear, colorless fuming liquid.
Molecular Weight	: 36.46
Specific Gravity	: 1.19
Solubility	: In water; miscible in all proportions with alcohol and water.

Maximum Limits of Impurities
Non-Volatile .... 0.0005 %
Free Chlorine (Cl) .... 0.0002 %
Sulphate (SO$_4$) .... 0.0002 %
Sulphite (SO$_2$) .... 0.003 %
Arsenic (As) 0.00001%
Iron (Fe) .... 0.0001 %
Other Heavy Metals (as Pb) .... 0.0005 %
Conforms to A.C.S. specifications.

Acid hydrochloric can be used in a developer in order that the Ph indication may be lowered. There will be an increase in contrast depending upon the amount of acid hydrochloric added to the solution. Acid Hydrochloric is one of the strongest inorganic acids known. Its salts are usually the most soluble, the outstanding exception being silver chloride, which particularly makes for interest in photography. Acid hydrochloric should be kept in well stoppered glass bottles at ordinary temperatures.

ACID LACTIC
CH$_3$CH.OH.COOH

Physical Characteristics :	Clear, colorless or slightly yellowish, odorless, syrupy, optically inactive liquid.
Molecular Weight	: 90.05
Specific Gravity	: 1.2485
Solubility	: In water, alcohol, and ether.

Maximum Limit of Impurities
Non-Volatile 0.020%
Chloride (Cl) 0.002%

127

Sulphate (SO_4)	0.005%
Iron (Fe)	0.001%
Other Heavy Metals (as Pb)	0.000%
Substances Darkened by H_2SO_4	Trace
Sugars	0.00 %

Acid lactic acts as a preservative for organic substances. In amidol developers, 5 ccs of acid lactic to 1000 ccs of developer will prevent the rapid deterioration of amidol. If the concentration of acid lactic is increased to 3%, it will act as an efficient stop bath and arrest development. This organic acid is more readily oxidizable than most organic acids used in photography. It is rather hygroscopic and should, therefore, be kept in tightly sealed dark bottles and protected from excessive light and heat.

ACID SALICYLIC
$C_6H_4OH \cdot COOH$

Physical Characteristics :	Fine, white, odorless, acicular crystals or crystalline powder.
Molecular Weight	: 138.05
Specific Gravity	: 1.483
Melting Point	: 158° Centigrade
Solubility	: In alcohol and ether; slightly soluble in water; highly soluble in 10% sodium sulphite solutions.

Maximum Limit of Impurities

Residue on Ignition	0.020%
Chloride (Cl)	0.002%
Sulphate (SO_4)	0.004%
Iron (Fe)	0.000%
Other Heavy Metals (as Pb)	0.000%

Acid salicylic is a preservative of organic substances. It is a fairly stable organic compound and changes slightly on exposure to air and light. It should be stored in dark bottles closely corked and away from metallic contacts. Acid salicylic has a tendency to prevent gelatin from absorbing water.

ALCOHOL ETHYL
C₂H₅OH

Physical Characteristics : Colorless, volatile, inflammable liquid. One of the outstanding major known solvents.

Molecular Weight : 46
Specific Gravity : .785
Freezing Point : -112.3° Centigrade
Boiling Point : 78.4° Centigrade

Alcohol ethyl is frequently added to photographic emulsions because it is a preservative and seems to exercise some control over silver halide grain. It is an excellent solvent for many organic substances.

ALCOHOL ISO-PROPYL
CH₃CHOHCH₃

Physical Characteristics : Colorless liquid somewhat resembling acetone. Used in the manufacture of intermediates.

Molecular Weight : 60.06

Alcohol iso-propyl is gradually becoming a favorite in developing formulas, due to its high solvent properties and penetration. 97-98% strength only is recommended for photographic use.

ALCOHOL METHYL
CH₃OH

Physical Characteristics : Clear, colorless, very mobile liquid; burns with a non-illuminating flame; has high solvent qualities.

Molecular Weight : 32.03
Specific Gravity : .7913
Freezing Point : -97.8° Centigrade
Boiling Point : 66.78° Centigrade
Solubility : In water, alcohol, and ether.

Non-Volatile .... 0.001 %
Precipitated by H_2O .... 0.000 %
Acetone, Aldeydes .... 0.000 %
Acidity (as $HC_2H_3O_2$) .... 0.003 %
Alkalinity (as NH_3) 0.0003%
Ethyl Alcohol ....abt. 1.
Subs Darkened by H_2SO_4 ....Passes A.C.S. test
Subs. Reducing $KMnO_4$ ....Passes A.C.S. test

Alcohol methyl or wood alcohol is not recommended for photographic use because of its tendency to produce fog in the developed image.

AMIDOL
(Diaminophenol HCl)
$C_6H_3(OH)(NH_2)_2,2HCl$

Physical Characteristics : Grayish white crystalline substance.

Molecular Weight   : 197.05

Solubility   : Easily soluble in w a t e r; slightly soluble in alcohol.

The importance of amidol over the other developers is that it can be used without any alkali. Amidol tends towards bluish blacks and is one of the most rapid developers known. It has thirty to forty times the reducing energy of hydroquinone. Amidol, which is usually used in acid solutions, tends to produce fine grain negatives. Apparently this acidity is important for these results.

Great care is necessary in the handling of amidol due to its extreme sensitivity to oxidation. Solutions should be prepared as needed because stock solutions lose their developing power within a few days. This oxidation takes place without any visible discoloration. The chemical itself should be kept tightly corked and away from heat and light.

AMMONIA WATER, 28%
(Ammonium Hydroxide, NH_4OH)

Physical Characteristics : Colorless liquid; i n t e n s e, pungent, suffocating odor; strong alkaline reaction.

Specific Gravity   : .897
26° Be minimum 27% NH3
Boiling Point   : 38.5° Centigrade
Solubility   : Miscible with all proportions
                         of water and alcohol.

Maximum Limits of Impurities

Non-Volatile .... 0.010 %
Carbon Dioxide (CO_2) .... 0.005 %
Chloride (Cl) 0.0001%
Phosphate (PO_4) .... 0.000 %
Sulphur Compounds (as SO_4) .... 0.001 %
Iron (Fe) 0.0002%
Other Heavy Metals (as Pb) 0.0005%
Pyridine .... 0.00 %
Subs. Reducing $KMnO_4$ .... 0.000 %

Ammonia water can be used as an accelerator of developing solutions. It is caustic and will therefore have
a tendency to enlarge the grain structure of a negative.
When speed is a primary consideration, films can be
placed in a closet and subjected to the fumes of ammonia water. This will hyper-sensitize the film and
increase its emulsion speed from 200-300%. There will
be a corresponding increase in the grain structure when
this is done. Avoid iodine, chlorine, acids and most
metallic salts. Caution: Keep cool in strong glass
stoppered bottles not completely filled.

AMMONIUM CARBONATE
$NH_4HCO_3 + NH_4NH_2CO_2$

Physical Characteristics : W h i t e, hard, translucent
                            lumps or cubes which lose
                            NH_3 and CO_2 on exposure to
                            air.
Molecular Weight   : 157
Melting Point   : 85° Centigrade
Solubility   : In 5 parts of water; decom-
                          poses in hot water.

Maximum Limit of Impurities

Residue on Ignition .... 0.010 %
Insoluble Matter .... 0.005 %
Chloride (Cl) 0.0005%
Phosphate (PO) 0.0005%

Sulphur Compounds (as SO) .... 0.002 %
Iron (Fe) 0.0005%
Other Heavy Metals (as Pb) 0.0005%
Conforms to A.C.S. specifications.

Ammonium carbonate may be used to replace potassium or sodium carbonate. It is difficult to keep this salt for any length of time without chemical changes taking place in it.

AMMONIUM CHLORIDE
NH₄Cl

Physical Characteristics : White odorless granules or powder.

Molecular Weight   : 53.50
Specific Gravity   : 1.520
Solubility   : In water, alcohol and ammonium hydroxide.

Maximum Limits of Impurities

Insoluble Matter .... 0.005 %
Residue on Ignition .... 0.010 %
Free Acid ....Passes A.C.S. Test
Phosphate (PO₄) 0.0002%
Sulphate (SO₄) .... 0.002 %
Sulphocyanate (CNS) .... 0.000 %
Arsenic (As) 0.0002%
Calcium and Magnesium Precip. .... 0.002 %
Iron (Fe) 0.005%
Other Heavy Metals (as Pb) 0.0005%
Conforms to A.C.S. specifications.

Ammonium chloride is used in fixing solutions in order to speed up the process of fixation. One of the unusual properties of this salt is that it sublimes without melting. When the fumes from hydrochloric acid and ammonia meet, they immediately form a white smoke which is ammonium chloride. This is a stable salt at ordinary temperatures. When NH₄CL is added to an alkaline solution, ammonia is liberated, thereby reducing the alkalinity.

FORMALDEHYDE
CH₂O

Physical Characteristics : Clear, colorless liquid of pungent odor.

Molecular Weight : 30.02
Specific Gravity : 1.075-1.081
Solubility : In water and alcohol.

Maximum Limit of Impurities

Non-Volatile .... 0.040 %
Acid (as CHOOH) .... 0.03 %
Chloride (Cl) .... 0.000 %
Sulphate (SO₄) .... 0.002 %
Iron (Fe) 0.0005%
Other Heavy Metals (as Pb) .... 0.000 %

A 10% solution of formaldehyde is used as a hardening bath immediately after fixing for both negatives and prints. Very small quantities of formaldehyde have the power to prevent swelling of gelatin so that the gelatin will withstand warm solutions. Formaldehyde should be kept in dark, tightly corked bottles. Usually formaldehyde contains small quantities of Formic acid which gives it an acid reaction. Normally formaldehyde is neutral in reaction. It is a powerful reducing agent. Silver nitrate will, under suitable conditions, be reduced to metallic silver.

GLYCERIN
$C_3H_5(OH)_3$

Physical Characteristics : Clear, colorless, syrupy liquid; absorbs moisture from the air.
Molecular Weight : 92.06
Specific Gravity : 1.2604
Melting Point : 17° Centigrade
Boiling Point : 290° Centigrade
Solubility : In water and alcohol; insoluble in ether.

Maximum Limit of Impurities

Non-Volatile .... 0.005 %
Chloride (Cl) 0.0005%
Sulphate (SO₄) .... 0.001 %
Ammonia (NH₃) .... 0.000 %
Arsenic (As) 0.0002%
Iron (Fe) .... 0.000 %
Other Heavy Metals (as Pb) .... 0.000 %

Acrolein & Sugars ....Not detectable
Fatty Acid Esters .... 0.05 %
Silver Reducing Substances .... None
Subs. Darkened by H_2SO_4 ....Passes test

Glycerin is used in fine grain developing solutions because of its ability to penetrate the emulsion and allow free access to the reducing agents. The life of a developing solution containing paraphenylenediamine will be materially reduced when glycerine is added to it. Glycerin is a popular solvent for many substances.

GLYCIN
(Paraoxyphenyl glycocoll)
$C_6H_4(OH)NH\ CH_2COOH$

Physical Characteristics : White to grayish brown substance. This substance is poisonous and should not be confused with the medicinal glycine which is chemically Amino Acetic acid.

Molecular Weight : 151.08

The use of glycin photographically is important in that it does not produce fog under prolonged use even in the absence of soluble bromide. It is noted as a fine grain developer. It keeps well in solution, and is therefore specifically recommended for continuous use in tank development. A glycin developer is slow but powerful.

HYDROQUINONE
$C_6H_4(OH)_2$

Physical Characteristics : White, colorless crystals.
Molecular Weight : 110.08
Melting Point : 170° Centigrade
Boiling Point : 285° Centigrade at 730 mm pressure.
Solubility : In 16 parts of water at 15° Centigrade; very soluble in alcohol and ether.

134

The developing properties of hydroquinone were discovered by Abney in 1880. Hydroquinone is rather a slow developer but it is noted for its strong contrast effects. It is seldom used alone due to its slow action, but is combined with other speedier developers. Its solution oxidizes very rapidly as will the crystals. Therefore both the solution and salt should be kept tightly corked and away from heat and light. At temperatures below 50° Fahrenheit, hydroquinone ceases to act.

METOL
$C_6H_4OH.NHCH_3$, ½ H_2SO_4
Mono Methyl Paramino Phenol Sulphate

Physical Characteristics : White, crystalline powder.
Molecular Weight   : 172.16
Melting Point   : 250°-260° Centigrade, with decomposition.
Solubility   : 1:20 in cold water; 1:6 in boiling water.

Metol was introduced commercially in 1891. Since then many American manufacturers have introduced this chemical under various trade names, such as Photol, Elon, et cetera. This type of organic compound is a mild reducing agent and possesses the property of developing exposed silver halide. Relative reducing energy of this compound as compared to hydroquinone as a standard is 20 to 1. Metol is seldom used alone but usually with hydroquinone or adurol. It is considered a soft working developer.

PARAPHENYLENEDIAMINE
Base ($C_6H_4(NH_2)_2$)

Physical Characteristics : Colorless to slightly reddish crystals.
Molecular Weight   : 108.11
Melting Point   : 140° Centigrade
Solubility   : In water, alcohol and ether; heat increases solubility to an unusually large extent.

PARAPHENYLENEDIAMINE
Hydrochloride ($C_6H_4(NH_2)_2 2HCl$)

Molecular Weight : 181.05

Solubility : Easily soluble in w a t e r; slightly soluble in alcohol and ether.

These substances have a very low reducing energy and are therefore slow developers. They are noted for production of fine grain images. They are practically devoid of contrast-giving properties. Both substances darken generally on exposure and should be kept in tightly corked containers away from light and heat.

POTASSIUM ALUM
$AlK(SO_4)_2.12H_2O$

Physical Characteristics : Large, colorless, hard, transparent crystals or white crystalline powder.

Molecular Weight : 474.41

Specific Gravity : 1.7571

Melting Point : 105° Centigrade

Solubility : In 8 parts cold water and equal parts in boiling water; insoluble in alcohol.

Maximum Limit of Impurities

Insoluble Matter	0.010 %
Chloride (Cl)	0.0005%
Ammonia (NH_3)	0.030 %
Arsenic (As)	0.0002%
Iron (Fe)	0.001 %
Other Heavy Metals (as Pb)	0.002 %

Potassium alum is used in hardening-fixing solutions because of its hardening effect upon gelatin. The hardening power of potassium alum is quickly exhausted by the presence of glycin and paraphenylenediamine in the solution. For this reason hardening-fixing baths containing potassium alum should be renewed frequently.

POTASSIUM BROMIDE
KBr

Physical Characteristics : Colorless crystals or white granules.
Molecular Weight : 119.02
Specific Gravity : 2.749
Melting Point : 730° Centigrade
Boiling Point : 1435° Centigrade
Solubility : In water; slightly soluble in ether and alcohol.

Maximum Limits of Impurities

Insoluble Matter .... 0.005 %
Alkalinity (as K CO) .... 0.005 %
Bromate (BrO) .... 0.001 %
Chloride (Cl) .... 0.40 %
Iodide (I) .... 0.00 %
Nitrogen Compounds (as N) .... 0.001 %
Sulphate (SO) .... 0.005 %
Barium (Ba) .... 0.002 %
Calcium, Magnesium and NH OH Precip. .... 0.005 %
Iron (Fe) 0.0005%
Other Heavy Metals (as Pb) 0.0005%

Conforms to A.C.S. specifications

Potassium bromide is added to developing solutions as a restrainer. Minute quantities of this chemical will eliminate fog in the emulsion and will decrease shadow detail causing more contrast. As the bromide is increased, the emulsion speed of the developer is decreased. Potassium bromide is rarely added to fine grain developers. This salt should be nearly free from copper and heavy metals.

POTASSIUM CARBONATE
K_2CO_3

Physical Characteristics : White, granular, deliquescent powder.
Molecular Weight : 138.20
Specific Gravity : 2.3312
Melting Point : 909° Centigrade
Boiling Point : Volatile at white heat.
Solubility : In water; insoluble in ether and alcohol.

Insoluble Matter .... 0.025 %
Moisture .... 2.000 %
Chloride and Chlorate (as Cl) .... 0.005 %
Nitrogen Compounds (as N) .... 0.002 %
Phosphate (PO_4) .... 0.005 %
Sulphur Compounds (as SO_4) .... 0.015 %
Arsenic (As) 0.0005%
Iron (Fe) .... 0.002 %
Other Heavy Metals (as Pb) 0.0005%

Potassium carbonate is used as an accelerator in certain developing formulas. It is also used as a neutralizer and dehydrating agent.

POTASSIUM METABISULPHITE
$K_2S_2O_5$

Physical Characteristics : Colorless, crystalline or white powder.

Molecular Weight   : 222.32

Solubility   : In water; insoluble in alcohol.

Chloride (Cl) .... 0.005 %
Arsenic (As) 0.0005%
Iron (Fe) .... 0.002 %
Other Heavy Metals (as Pb) .... 0.002 %

Potassium metabisulphite is used as a preservative in developers and for acidulating hypo baths. Its principal use is as an addition to pyro developers in order to preserve and to prevent excessive oxidation of the pyro. At times potassium metabisulphite is used in place of sodium sulphite and in several popular developing formulas is recommended along with sodium sulphite.

SODIUM BISULPHITE
$NaHSO_3$

Physical Characteristics : White, crystalline powder; faint sulphur dioxide odor.

Molecular Weight   : 104

Melting Point   : Decomposes

Solubility   : In water; insoluble in alcohol.

Chloride (Cl)	0.010%
Arsenic (As)	0.000%
Iron (Fe)	0.002%
Other Heavy Metals (as Pb)	0.002%

Sodium bisulphite is used for preserving organic reducing substances in developers. It is used also in the ordinary acid fixing baths. It should be nearly free from iron and copper. Metabisulphite, which is sometimes found in sodium bisulphite, causes decomposition of the hypo solution. Sodium bisulphite is a strong reducing agent and is incompatible with acids and oxidizers.

SODIUM BORATE
$Na_2B_4O_7.10H_2O$

Physical Characteristics	: White, hard prismatic crystals or fine powder.
Molecular Weight	: 381.43
Solubility	: In water and glycerin; insoluble in alcohol.

Maximum Limits of Impurities

Insoluble Matter	0.005 %
Carbonate (CO_2)	0.00 %
Chloride (Cl)	0.001 %
Phosphate (PO_4)	0.001 %
Sulphate (SO_4)	0.005 %
Arsenic (As)	0.0003%
Calcium (Ca)	0.005 %
Iron (Fe)	0.002 %
Other Heavy Metals (as Pb)	0.001 %

Conforms to A.C.S. specifications

Sodium borate is used as an accelerator in some developing formulas. Aqueous solutions of sodium borate are slightly alkaline. It is often used as a buffer to maintain a mild alkalinity in photographic solutions.

Sodium Carbonate, Monohydrate
$Na_2CO_3.H_2O$

Physical Characteristics	: White, odorless granular or crystalline powder; effloresces in warm dry air.
Molecular Weight	: 124.02

Solubility   : In 3 parts of water and in 7 parts of glycerin.

Sodium carbonate is the alkali generally used in developing solutions. It is not recommended in fine grain developing solutions because of its tendency to cause turbulence in the emulsion during the process of development, which results in a coarse grain structure. It should be free from caustic. It is incompatible with acids. The monohydrate is generally preferred to the anhydrous and decahydrate because of higher stability. On account of its adverse effect on the fine grain structure of the negative, some operators have tried other substances with much success.

SODIUM SULPHATE

$$Na_2SO_4 + 10H_2O$$

Physical Characteristics : Colorless crystals
Molecular Weight   : 322.21
Solubility   : In 3 parts of water; insoluble in alcohol; the solution is neutral to litmus paper.

Sodium sulphate is used in developers whenever it is necessary to develop at temperatures exceeding 74° Fahrenheit. Its action is to inhibit or delay swelling of the gelatin for a period generally long enough for the development process to be completed. Either the crystalline or anhydrous salt can be used in their proper proportions. Many alkaline salts will act likewise, but this one seems to be the favorite.

SODIUM SULPHITE

$$Na_2SO_3$$

Physical Characteristics : White, crystalline powder; a very strong reducing agent.
Molecular Weight   : 126.05

Solubility   : In 4 parts of water; insoluble
                                    in alcohol.

Maximum Limit of Impurities

Insoluble Matter .... 0.01 %
Free Acid .... None
Free Alkali (as Na_2CO_3) .... 0.3 %
Chloride (Cl) .... 0.020 %
Thiosulphate ....Not detectable
Arsenic (As) 0.0002%
Iron (Fe) .... 0.001 %
Other Heavy Metals (as Pb) .... 0.001 %

Conforms to A.C.S. specifications

Sodium sulphite is used in practically all developing
formulas because of its tremendous affinity for oxygen.
The action of this chemical is to absorb the oxygen in
both the air and water and oxidize itself to sodium sulphate. In the form of sodium sulphate it is inert. In
absorbing the oxygen, sodium sulphite preserves the organic reducing substances in the developer from oxidation. Another theory is that it forms a complex salt
with the developer which is less subject to oxidation
than either alone. Sodium sulphite is one of the important chemicals that particularly require careful selection, handling, and storing. It should be kept in
fairly small air-tight containers away from light and
heat, without metallic or caustic contamination.

SODIUM THIOSULPHATE
$Na_2S_2O_3.5H_2O$

Physical Characteristics : Colorless, slightly efflorescent
                            crystalline compound.
Molecular Weight   : 248.19
Specific Gravity   : 1.729
Melting Point   : 48° Centigrade
Boiling Point   : Decomposes
Solubility   : In water and oil of turpen-
                          tine; insoluble in alcohol.

Hypo is the common name used among photographers for sodium thiosulphate. Its use as a fixing bath is
based on the fact that the hypo solution dissolves the
silver halides which have not been affected by the ac-

tion of light. Better grades of hypo have been obtained recently due to improved methods of manufacture. Clean hypo is important, and care in keeping it in clean containers is recommended.

Water

By reason of its extensive solvent powers not only of solids but also of gases, water generally becomes contaminated with foreign matter even under great care. Distillation is the usual method employed for purification even to the extent of three or more distillations for complete purity. The solvent powers afterward, however, even extend to dissolve parts of the containers it is kept in.

The principal interest of water in photography is its purity. Redistilled water is indicated and should be kept in glass containers that have little free alkali content. Where distilled water is not practically obtainable, natural soft water can be used because it does not contain as many impurities as ordinary water and can be tested by its readiness to make a lather with soap. Hard water is a variety which contains calcium or magnesium salts or other alkalis. Most of the public drinking waters are chlorinated for antiseptic and health purposes and, of course, are contraindicated for photographic uses.

ADVERTISEMENTS

144

CONTAX III

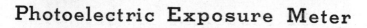

With Built-in
Photoelectric Exposure Meter

● Contax III represents the latest development in 35 mm. cameras. Embodied within this universal camera are means for instantly and accurately determining correct exposure and focus . . . the twin factors in assuring good negatives.

See the Contax III at your dealers. Write for booklet.

the Universal Camera

149